With the Mounted Infantry in South Africa

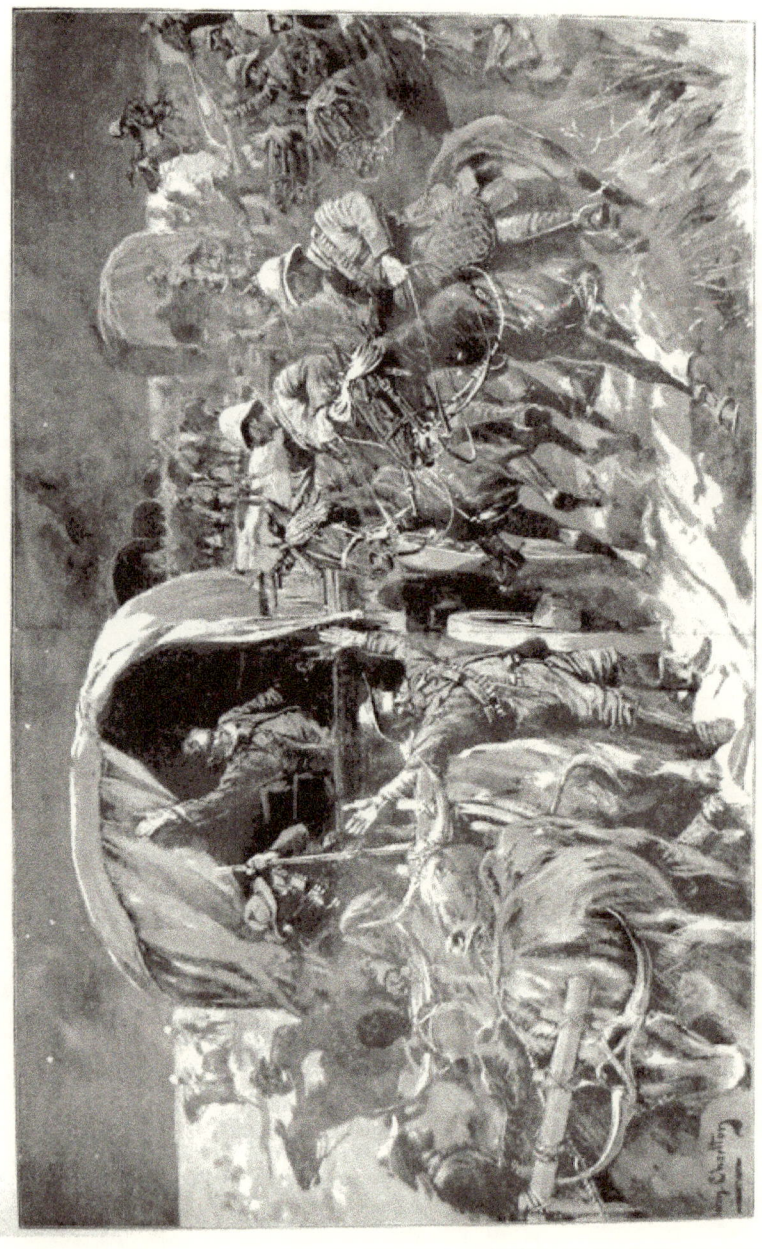

With the Mounted Infantry in South Africa
The Experiences of a Captain of the King's Royal Rifles M.I. During the Boer War

Frederick Maurice Crum

With the Mounted Infantry in South Africa
The Experiences of a Captain of the King's Royal Rifles M.I. During the Boer War
by Frederick Maurice Crum

First published under the title
With the Mounted Infantry in South Africa

Leonaur is an imprint of Oakpast Ltd
Copyright in this form © 2011 Oakpast Ltd

ISBN: 978-0-85706-755-5 (hardcover)
ISBN: 978-0-85706-756-2 (softcover)

http://www.leonaur.com

Publisher's Notes

The opinions of the authors represent a view of events in which he was a participant related from his own perspective, as such the text is relevant as an historical document.

The views expressed in this book are not necessarily those of the publisher.

Contents

Note	7
Talana and Dundee Hospital	9
Departure From Dundee Hospital	32
From Release, June 5th, 1900, to Rejoining Regiment, October 4th, 1900	53
October 9th, 1900, to February 1st, 1901	63
February 1st to April 27th, 1901	79
Lydenburg, April 28th to October 12th, 1901	111
Colonel Benson's Column	116
Colonel Mackenzie's Column	128

Note

The following pages have been printed from my diary, and from letters written home during the war in South Africa. I shall be I pleased if they are found in any way interesting to friends, notwithstanding the great number of accounts which have already appeared.

F. M. C

Malta,
Jan. 1903.

Part 1

Talana and Dundee Hospital

The detachment of the 1st Batt. King's Royal Rifles to which I belonged had been stationed in South Africa since January, 1896, so that when the war did come, in 1899, it was no surprise to us. Indeed, on our departure from India, many men were heard to express their intention of "pulling Mr. Kruger's whiskers," and very soon after our arrival at the Cape we started field days and training in South African warfare. General Sir Wm. Goodenough fully realised the possibility of war with the Boers, and trained the troops under him particularly in stalking and shooting, which he foresaw would be so important; yet, being anxious to do nothing in the way of hurrying matters, he used the term "South African" warfare, and forbad the words "Boer" warfare.

General Goodenough was succeeded by Colonel Morgan-Crofton, and later by Sir William Butler, and they too kept the troops employed, laying particular stress on the necessity for intelligence in individuals and on good shooting and stalking. So convinced were all ranks that they were training for the real thing, that we listened keenly, and profited greatly from serving under these commanders.

On May 5th, 1899, great excitement and a feeling of a coming ultimatum were caused by the correspondence between Mr, Chamberlain and Mr. Reitz. On Sunday, May 7th, we sailed from Cape Town, and joined the other four companies of the battalion at Maritzburg under Lieut.-Col. Gunning, arriving there on the night of May 11th. At Maritzburg we were kept busy soldiering, and all ranks showed a keenness which could only be inspired by the conviction that war was coming. It took a long time coming. For about four months we were in a continual state of suspense, We rushed at the morning papers every day—when the news looked like peace we were greatly depressed; when war seemed certain we were in tremendous spirits. We congratulated ourselves on being one of the regiments on the spot, and our only regret was lest someone should have to be left behind.

In June Sir William Penn Symonds, from India, took over the command in Natal. He kept us busy with constant field days, taking a special interest in the Mounted Infantry, to which I belonged. He was a keen and capable soldier, and though some of us thought that his tactics were more suited for Afridis than for Boers, yet we all felt that he was a leader of men, and all were ready to go anywhere with him.

In June and July I made expeditions to the neighbourhood of Laing's Nek, for a fight there was looked upon in those days as a certainty, and it would be a great advantage to know the ground. The historical interest of the ride along the Nek from Majuba to the Buffalo was greatly added to by the feeling that we might someday soon be either attacking the south side or resisting an attack from the north. The feeling on the border was already strained, and there was considerable uneasiness at Charlestown, where, I remember, there was a meeting of the residents to discuss what they should do in the event of war, should Charlestown not be held by our troops. A retirement on Newcastle was decided on by all the residents except one, an old soldier, who voted for forming a laager and resisting to the end.

On the night of Sunday, Sept 24th, General Symonds came in to us while we were all at mess. We all stopped talking, and felt that something was up. The general said that we were to move up next day to Ladysmith, while the Ladysmith garrison was being moved on to Dundee. This looked like business at last. The battalion went up by train, while the Mounted Infantry Company marched up the road with the 5th Lancers. The enthusiasm was tremendous, and I shall never forget the exchanges of cheering which took place when we, marching north by road, met the crowded trains of refugees coming south by rail from Johannesburg.

A fine serviceable looking lot were these troops, and, looking back on them now, I feel sure that better never started for the front than the highly-trained troops which found themselves in the country at the beginning of the war. In those days there were a few, but very few, who would shake their heads and say that the Boer was a very good fighting man, that he was well armed, and that there was room for anxiety about the result. But we felt full of confidence; we expected to have one hard fight, perhaps two; and we realised that with modern quick-firing rifles there must be many casualties. But we were not going to make the blunders of 1880; we were dressed in khaki now, and well practiced in skirmishing. We would be in Johannesburg by Christmas.

On October 1st we reached Colenso. While we encamped there, detachments of the Natal Carabineers, Durban Light Infantry, and the Natal Naval Volunteers, with two guns, arrived to do garrison duty. All were keen for a fight, and regretting that they should be thus employed on lines of communication. It makes one smile now to think of the two old 40-pounder muzzle-loading guns, which had been solemnly brought up from Durban to Colenso to be pitted against the Boer Long Toms.

In peace time Ladysmith as a military station had always had a bad name. Officers had been known to resign their commissions rather than serve there, and when we arrived there, as we did on a typical afternoon, on October 2nd, we were well able to realise why Ladysmith was unpopular. Wherever one went the dust was ankle deep, a black, grimy dust, which was blown by strong hot winds for the first half of the day in one direction, and then, at half time, the wind would change and blow the whole lot back again. The flies were so thick that one could not eat without swallowing them, and the heat was most oppressive. Very glad we were when on October 4th orders came for us to march to Dundee next day. Colonel Gunning had been asked how long it would take him to start for Dundee, and he had answered like a good rifleman, "I am ready now, Sir," with the result that we were chosen to go instead of another regiment which had been intended for Dundee.

Our last night at Ladysmith was a real bad one. All tents had been struck and packed on the waggons, and we were sleeping in the open, when a storm and whirlwind of dust came along our way, carrying off boots, helmets, and kits into the darkness. As we started before daylight we were unable to retrieve everything, and some who had taken great care to provide themselves with complete campaigning kits started at the very outset with incomplete ones.

The Leicester Regiment, two Batteries R.F.A., and the 18th Hussars, under Colonel Moller, had already reached Dundee, and had reported being fired on in the Glencoe Pass; and there were rumours of a concentration of 16,000 Boers on the Border. Our party consisted of the 1st Batt. K.R.R., Major Wing's Battery R.F.A., and our Company of M.I. (96 men under Captain Northey), the whole under Colonel Gunning. Full military precautions were taken, our company doing the scouting, and we arrived at Dundee without adventure on the afternoon of Saturday, October 7th.

Dundee, with its beautiful climate and scenery, was much appreciated after Ladysmith. Though we knew that there were large numbers of armed Boers collected near the borders, still there was a feeling that war was by no means certain, even up to October 11th, when the Boers celebrated Kruger's birthday by firing in their ultimatum, and thus removed all doubt. In those days, with the Dundee shops all open, and the civilians carrying on their ordinary pursuits, while our bands played regularly each afternoon, it was difficult to realise that fighting was so imminent.

About October 10th General Symonds arrived and took over the command; later Colonel Yule arrived, and soon all the women and children were sent down country. Rumours grew more and more serious, till at last, on October 12th (my birthday), we heard that the Boers had declared war. Shots had been fired near Van Reenen's Pass, and large numbers of Boers were advancing from all directions. At the time I heard the news, I was writing a letter home. Though so long expected, it came as a shock. I sat up with a start and thought, "Well, now we are in for a big thing." On October 13th we woke to find that the whole battalion of Dublin Fusiliers had been sent down to Ladysmith. The Free State Boers were expected in the direction of Van Reenen's Pass. As they had already 8000 troops at Ladysmith, and we had only 3000 at Dundee, and as they had not so many Boers to deal with as we had, we grudged losing our old friends the Dublin Fusiliers. However, they soon came back; so when, on the 16th the Royal Irish Fusiliers under Colonel Carleton also joined us, we felt ready for all comers.

From the 12th to the 19th the scouting by day and the picquets by night kept the mounted troops hard at work. These parties were sent out to considerable distances, far further than would have been considered advisable later in the war; however, they never came to any harm, and even the night picquet of twelve men under Lieutenant Grimshaw, Dublin Fusiliers, three miles east of camp, which was rushed at 3 a.m. the morning of Talana, had only one man wounded; the rest succeeded in falling back and warning General Symonds of the attack.

On October 18th I had been out from 4 a.m. to 6 p.m., doing a hard day's reconnoitring with four picked men of the M.I., one Natal *carabineer*, a man called Spencer, with a good head and local knowledge, and one police trooper, who also knew the district We had been sent to watch the Landsman and Laffine's Drifts over the Buffalo, about twelve miles from camp. To do this we had stalked up by Fort Pine to the top of Moma Mountain, and then worked our way along the Malmgave Range, fully expecting to see something of a party of thirty Boers who were daily in those parts. There were none, however, that day, so after waiting till 3 p.m. at a place where we could see several of the drifts over the Buffalo, we left for camp, calling at the Wade's Farm on the way.

On arrival in camp I reported to General Symonds, who had trustworthy news that the Boers were all round us and intended to attack next day. He seemed relieved to hear it was all clear in the direction I had come from.

We were joined this day by Stuart Wortley, Jelf, and Johnson, who had come in a cruiser from Cape Town just in time.

The long day's reconnoitring upset me, and I spent a bad night. I had to remain in bed with fever the following day, and very glad I was that the expected battle did not come off just then.

On Friday, October 20th, the troops fell in at 5 a.m. awaiting an attack. I lay awake on my valise listening, and praying that the Boers would give me yet another day to get fit in. Dr. Julien passed my tent and told me on no account to get up, I told him the blister he had put on me had made me so sore, and the fever had left me so weak, that I didn't think I should do the Boers much harm, but that if they did come, I should certainly have a try. At 5.15 a.m. all our fellows came back much disappointed, saying the battle was "off" again. The troops had been dismissed, and it looked like another day of "armed peace." Presently I heard a rumour that Grimshaw and his picquet of twelve men of M.I. had been rushed.

Next I heard the mess servants outside my tent say, "What's them 'ere bloaks on that bloomin' hill?" and some discussion as to whether they were Boers or Dublin Fusiliers. Going out of my tent I saw them looking at the hill above Piet Smith's Farm, which is about two miles east of the town, I saw crowds of men on the sky-line, and something very like guns. The whole camp had turned out to look at them. I felt that they were Boers at once, rushed into my tent, and forgetting my fever and blister and everything else, bundled on my clothes as fast as ever I could. I had got one *puttee* on and was just putting on the other, when there was a loud, sharp report from the hill, a noise like a rocket travelling through the air, then a thud, and an explosion, which sounded at the next tent.

Never did I spend less time dressing than that morning, and yet I forgot none of the things which I should need for a long day's fighting—my difficulty was to find them. Every coat but the right one seemed to come to hand. Another shell, close to, nearly made me put on Northey's coat, but just in time I saw mine bang at the bottom of everything. "Where are my field glasses, my watch, my knife, my whistle and helmet?" More shells tell me I must not waste time; luckily there is my haversack full of necessary articles, and my sword-belt, but of course, that is buckled up and wants a lot of undoing.

"Shall I take my sword? No, it won't be much use against Mausers. Spurs, too, can go to the devil. Well, here goes!" and I bolt across to the Mounted Infantry lines. The camp has been surprised; there is great confusion, but all are doing their best to get right. Shells are landing all over the camp— there goes one into a span of mules, but they don't seem to be killed. My men are saddling up quick as they can, some calm, some excited.

"Can I help you there? Your horse don't seem to like shells, but that's no reason for putting in the bit upside down, and that strap first—there—that's all right, up you get"

What a lot of loose horses!—hope mine are not loose. "Faulkner! Oh, there you are."

The good Faulkner with 'Rounie' and 'Fiddlehead' nearly ready—as cool as when saddling up in the paddock for a race; just a *soupçon* of excitement as he tells me my rein is twisted. "The 'Mounted' are going in that direction, Sir, I don't know what their orders are."

"All right, come on!" and away we go.

As I rode through the tents of our battalion I saw men huddled in twenties behind the tents, and just as I passed Colour-Sergeant Davies and B Company, one shell seemed to land right in the middle of some men, and yet no great harm was done. The fire is very straight; how awful it would be if they fired shrapnel shells! I felt so sorry for our men having to sit still and do nothing, and I rather felt riding away from them into comparative safety. At first, I am told, there was just the least tendency to panic, but the regiment which had faced death quietly on the *Warren Hastings* was soon steadied.

"Now then, D Company!" from Jack Pechell, and "Steady, men!" from Johnny Campbell, and every man was sitting tight, hoping for luck and waiting for orders. The Mounted Infantry, with the 18th Hussars and all the pack and transport animals, had orders to get under cover under the rocky slope to the north side of the camp. It must have been about 6.15 a.m. when all were present and formed up. With our Company there were Northey, Jelf, Majendie, myself and about eighty men. We went round and saw that each man had his ammunition, his magazine charged with ten rounds, and food in his haversack. All the men were ready and keen. I told my lot that all I wanted of them was to keep cool and shoot straight.

As we had no orders, I got leave from Northey to ask the general what our orders were. The artillery duel had begun. Our guns had got a bad start; all their horses were away watering, so that they could not choose their positions, and had to fire from where they were. But they were three grand batteries; every shot they fired was a good shot, and gave confidence to our side, while it told on the enemy.

General Symonds and his staff were standing at his tent near the guns when I galloped up. Shells seemed to be visiting this neighbourhood too. The general signed to me not to gallop, and asked, "Well, what is it?" I told him the Dublin and Rifles M.I. had no orders. He said, "You are to go with the 18th Hussars. Go and tell Colonel Moller that he is to wait under cover—it may be for one or two hours—and I will send him word to advance, but he may advance if he sees a good opportunity. Go quietly, don't gallop." I repeated the order clearly to the general to make sure I had it correctly. I trotted away to where the horses were, told Lonsdale and Northey, and then told Colonel Moller, The whole lot then dismounted.

Knowing that much larger forces were to be expected from the direction of Impati than from the Buffalo, I felt very uneasy about what was now our left flank. The early morning mists had not yet cleared from the ridge, and the top of Impati was in a cloud, I got leave to ride out, while we were waiting, to have a look in that direction.

I took one man (Swaine) with me and galloped about two miles to the top of the ridge above Seager's Farm, on the road to Hatting Spruit. Finding all clear, we turned round and headed across country towards Indumeni, and made for some mounted men a mile or two from camp, towards Glencoe. As we crossed the Sand Spruit, we watered our horses, and I took a drink, as I was feeling very dry. We found it was the Leicester M.I. we had seen. We talked to some gunners who were there with the R.A. transport, and then rode back to the Company. Perhaps this bit of scouting was rather officious, but I was young, and was just as well employed thus perhaps as doing nothing. It was from the same ridge, on the Hatting Spruit road, that

Erasmus's guns and Joubert's commando attacked the next day.

It must have been nearly 8 a.m. when I got back to Colonel Moller and the 18th Hussars. He told me our M.I. had gone on with the 18th's maxim gun, so I galloped on after them. I soon came in sight of them working down the Sand Spruit valley, and getting round the Boer's right. There was also one squadron of cavalry. The enemy's guns on Smith's Kop, or Talana Hill, had spotted this move, and opened fire on the moving target As Swaine and I drew nearer the maxim, we got nearer the shell fire. I said to him, "Don't ride beside me; there is no reason why we should both get shot" He said he could not hold his bally horse, so I took a pull at mine and let him shoot about ten yards ahead.

Immediately afterwards a shell whistled past between us and struck the bank of the stream close to us I had hardly time to say "By Jove!" when another, and then a third fell, all so close that one felt it was a question of inches. This was their quick-firing gun, afterwards known as the pom-pom, which had evidently got the range, if not the direction, of our maxim gun. I got up to our maxim, and found that my section of M.I. were not there, only twenty-two men, under Majendie, as escort. The men of this escort were far too close together, but we got them to open out after a lot of shouting. The 18th squadron had gone on in front There were a lot of wire fences, which we cut in several places. Crossing the Sand Spruit, we halted a few minutes in the river bed, and here I got Majendie to give me half his men, so we advanced in two small sections, each under an officer. When men are excited or under fire, I should say from the experience of this day that twelve men is as many as one man can supervise.

Once round the Boer flank, the firing on us ceased, and one had more time to look to one's front and left. The front was clear enough, but the hills covered with mist on our left might have held an Army Corps. We pushed on down the left bank of the Sand Spruit, through two farms and a *kraal* and more barbed wire fences, then, turning sharp to the right, we re-crossed the *spruit* at a bad place, and came right up under cover of a ridge of stones and boulders on the Meyer's Drift road, where it looks down on Schultz's Farm. Here we found the advanced squadron of the 18th Hussars. Soon afterwards we were joined by the remainder of the 18th and the whole company of Dublin Fusiliers M.I., who had also been heavily fired at from Talana on their way. There was cover here for all, so we dismounted and waited.

I crept up to where Colonel Moller was, and asked leave to have

Hussar advanced guard discovering the enemy

a look over the ridge. It was grand—here we were on the Boers' right rear, at about 1500 to 2000 yards range, with a maxim gun, 120 rifles, and a whole regiment of cavalry. The hill the Boers were on commanded us by about 500 feet, but we were out of sight and under cover from them. Their pom-pom was quiet now, and the other Boer guns did not seem so busy. Peeping up I could see fully 500 ponies, and a lot of Boers. What was the range? Major Greville put it at 1200 yards, but I put it at 2000. We asked for a range-finder, but there was none, we had all come out in such a hurry. But we should soon get the range when we began firing. We had a grand chance if we only waited and kept out of sight The only question to my mind was whether we ought to leave our horses and go slap bang at them, or fire from where we were when the proper time came.

The ground all round our ridge was bare and open, and by shifting a few rocks and boulders, we very soon had a strong position against an attack. It must have been about 11 a.m. Our guns seemed to have nearly silenced theirs, and the time to fire must have been about ripe, when the colonel sent out a squadron towards Dr. Schultz's Farm, and soon afterwards took the maxim gun and the whole of the rest of his force in that direction—what his reason was I can't say—it was a very great disappointment to me. We went on, cutting fences as we went, about two miles, till we came on the Landsman Drift road. There the M.I. were ordered to dismount, and extend along at right angles to the road, facing the Boers' rear. We were behind the centre of the Boer position, and about two-and-a-half miles from it The country here is open and undulating, covered with thousands of ant-heaps. We lined out across the road, every man behind his ant-heap, our whole line being about half-a-mile long. Our horses were in a slight hollow, about 400 yards in rear.

Here we lay for about an hour, doing nothing. What our object in coming was, I don't know. Hidden on a flank this small force might have been of some use when the Boers retreated, but what was the use of planting 120 men across the line of retreat of 4000? While waiting, I had a good opportunity of watching the Boer position and movements. They occupied three distinct hills. Their right was on Talana Hill, an isolated hill about 600 feet high; their centre on a similar hill about 700 feet high, being a spur of the Lennox Hill. Both these were steep and bare, and almost impregnable. Through the pass they form, runs the road from Dundee to all the drifts over the Buffalo River. The third hill, to the Boer left and drawn back, was the Lennox Hill itself. The Lennox Hill was occupied by about 2000 Boers; it afforded the Boers a good line of retreat, and closed our line of retreat by the Helpmakaar Road.

Looking at Talana Hill from my position in the rear, I could see a farmhouse with a huge ambulance flag; this was the Boer Hospital, to which I was taken later. There were still hundreds of Boers and ponies moving about near the farm. These were probably skulking under the protection of the red-cross flag. At the same time I saw one or two of our shells burst over the top of the hill; I could not make out what had happened. On the centre hill I could see crowds of horses and men, about 2000; the horses looked like flocks of sheep or goats on the side of the hill. I longed to see some of our shells planted among them, and all but sent a messenger round to tell the colonel of the artillery about them. On Lennox Hill, a large force was collecting, another 2000 I thought The whole force I put down at about 5000, and from conversations I have had since with various Boers, I think that estimate is about right.

After about an hour a rumour came of an attack on our rear. We were ordered back to our horses, and mounted, but it turned out to be a false alarm. After this we changed our position, still more to the Boer left, and lined out as before, but facing Lennox Hill. I saw a move of some kind going on on Lennox Hill. The Boers were leaving Talana and making for Lennox Hill. I can't say what time this was, but should think it was nearly 2 p.m. A party of about 200 was moving from Lennox Hill in our direction. I went along our line till I came to Lonsdale, and pointed out this move to him. He and I, with his collie dog, walked out some way to the front to look at the ground, and choose a better position to meet this advance. This open ground, covered with ant-heaps, is very deceptive—one keeps on seeing just in front of one what looks like a good position, but when you get there you find it does not command the clear view it seemed to, and that lying down you can only see a short distance ahead.

The ground we were on sloped towards a water-course or *donga*, about a mile distant. The Boers were advancing down to this water-course in a straight line for us. Later the whole of the 2000 on Lennox Hill also took this line. I think now this was the beginning of the Boer retirement, but at the time I sent Faulkner to tell Colonel Moller they were going to attack us. I remember that we called for a range-finder again, but could only get one box, and that the wrong one. We moved the line up a bit, bringing the right forward. The maxim under Cape,

18th Hussars, was on the left behind two large ant-heaps, the Dublin M.I. in the centre, and we on the right I felt that we were now in for our first experience of Mauser bullets.

Walking down our line, I cautioned each man not to fire unless he could see something to fire at; not to waste a single round, and to keep his magazine for an emergency, I was sorry I had not got my own men, though I knew these men pretty well. Someone called to me, "They are firing on the left, Sir," and, looking towards Lennox Hill, I could see the whole Boer force coming towards us. The Dublins had opened fire on them. They were firing very quickly on the left, "independent." The range was over a mile, which in those days was considered almost out of range. However, it was a large target and a good opportunity, so I fired a couple of volleys before they were lost sight of in the *donga*.

But the other Boers, whom we had first seen advancing towards us, were considerably nearer now. Bullets began to whistle past us, and the men were taking every advantage of the ant-heaps. "Shoot whenever you can see anything to shoot at!—no Hythe words of command"—I yelled. The maxim was blazing away, the Dublins were having a great fusillade, and the Boer bullets were more and more plentiful; but I could see nothing to fire at, and even standing up I could only occasionally catch sight of a Boer creeping towards an ant-heap. I could see several horses, and there were a good many galloping about loose. Our men were very cool and steady. The fire was getting very warm, very straight; this really was business. I was not the least afraid of them in front, but they were certain to work round us before long, and our horses, about 250 yards in the rear, were quite exposed enough already.

I found one of our men lying behind an ant-heap, thinking more of cover than of shooting. I took his rifle. "You must shoot, man!" I said, and with his rifle I had about five shots and left him, saying, "Why can't you do that yourself.?" Another man seemed much excited, and I had a shot or two out of his rifle to steady him. I knew the Boer, once ensconced behind his ant-heap, would not come nearer than a hundred yards so long as we kept up the fire, but I felt most anxious all the time about my right flank.

"The Dublins have retired, sir."

"All right," I answered, "hang on a bit longer; keep up the fire,"—then, after a short space to cover their retirement—"*Now!*" I shouted, "one volley along the ground, and then join the horses. *Volleys! Ready!*

Along the ground! Present! Fire! Retire!" There was a lull in the Boers' fire, and then a perfect hail of bullets followed us as we ran back to our horses and mounted. Wonderful that we don't seem to be getting hit, I thought, when poor Greenfield's horse carried him past me; he was hit in the middle of the back, and done for. I think it was here that Williams and Cullam were hit too. The Dublins and the maxim were well away; so, telling my men to follow them, I made for the colonel to ask him for orders. I told him the Boers were getting round me and I had had to retire. I asked for orders.

"Go and hold that ridge, and cover my retirement" he said, pointing towards Schultz's Farm. The cavalry had been doing nothing all this time, and I was hoping they would have charged.

It was at this stage that Cape got cut off with his maxim gun. It was a most unfortunate thing, the only redeeming feature being the plucky way in which Cape and his six men stuck to their gun, when they might well have got away. Four of the men were killed, while Cape and the other two men were all three wounded and taken. I saw the dead bodies lying in the dry bed of the Sand Spruit, as I was brought back in the moonlight that night. I hope that a stone may someday be put up to mark the site of this plucky stand.

I galloped back, and passing Lonsdale, shouted my orders to him. When we got to the ridge we dismounted and held it, but only for a short time. There was a strong party of Boers heading to cut us off, and we were under a heavy fire from the Boers following us up. My chief thought was to get before the Boers to the ridge we had first left early that morning, and ought never to have left. I felt that once there we could stop any number of Boers, while if they got there first we were quite cut off, and the left flank of our main attack exposed. But the colonel, who now led the retirement, kept bearing off to the right, making straight for the north end of Impati Mountain. The retirement had a bad effect upon the men. We must have galloped a mile without a stop, and it was only with very great difficulty that Majendie and I could keep our men together and stop them going too fast. They were beginning to think they were being chased, whereas the shots were getting fewer and fewer, and there was every minute less reason for retiring.

Here it was that I took my knock. We halted behind a ridge, about one mile from Jordaan's Farm, dismounted, faced about and advanced in extended order, the Dublin Company on our right. At the top of the ridge we came under fire. I suppose there were some thirty fir-

Hussar scout at bay

ing at us now, but the Boers are so clever behind ant-heaps that there might have only been two or three. I took the two men on the left, and with them crept round the flank of the only two Boers I could see. We got well round them. I took a rifle from one of the men, and was standing up to take a steady aim at a Boer behind a heap not fifty yards away, when from another heap still closer a man fired and got me plump in the right shoulder. The rifle dropped with a thud, "Take the bally gun and shoot," I said, and turning back made straight for Faulkner, who held my pony three hundred yards in rear.

As I went the pain was very great; I thought my arm had been shot clean off, and was only hanging by a few threads of my khaki jacket. I seemed to be carrying in my left arm an enormous heavy bolster. The fingers were twitching and dancing, and seemed to be far away. I caught at them, and said goodbye to them affectionately. I realised that in this steeplechase of war I had come down at the first fence. When I reached Faulkner, he got his field-dressing at once, and tied it up as tight as he could pull at the shoulder joint. I was feeling very giddy. A doctor turned up almost immediately, a jolly good doctor too. He put me under the cover of an ant-heap, and disregarding all cover himself, cut off my jacket and shirt and dressed my wound. Just after this the order was given to retire, and they retired, leaving Dr. Hardy, his orderly (Private José, 18th Hussars), and me.

There were still occasional shots coming over us, and if we stayed where we were, the chances were that we should get between two fires. It was quite likely, too, that some Boer coming up might in his excitement have a shot at us. It was a job shifting out of our unsafe position, but once out of the fire and in Hardy's hands I felt much better. In the meantime the Boer advance seemed to have stopped—they never came beyond the point where I was hit. Why then were our people still retiring? I could see them disappearing over the ridge to the north of Impati, right into the arms of General Joubert's commandos which were known to be in that direction. About 220 strong they went on past the Impati, and lost their way in the direction of Hatting Spruit. They were attacked by the Ermelo and Pretoria commandos, and after a stand of two hours at a farm, against heavy guns and Mausers, the white flag was put up. No men could have behaved better than our twenty-two M.I. men did that day, eight of their number being hit; they deserved a better fate.

When Hardy had patched me up, he went back in the direction we had come from to look for more wounded, and I was left with

José to try and reach the nearest farm. All that day and the following night Hardy was working hard with the wounded, and whether it was a British soldier or a Boer Burgher, he treated all with the same care and kindness. Many of our men and many of the Boers, among them Drs. Van der Merve and Molloy of the Dutch Ambulance, have spoken to me since of Dr. Hardy and the good work he did.

With some difficulty José and I managed to reach the farmhouse. We were met by a most unsympathetic looking Dutchman, who at first seemed to have no intention of taking me in, but as I had neither the ability to go a yard further nor the intention of doing so, and as José ordered him to go and fetch some rugs for me, I was soon lying on the floor of his kitchen. It turned out to be Jordaan's Farm. He and his wife, a grown-up daughter, and two small children were the occupants. They could not speak English. Later a trooper of the 18th Hussars (Masters) was brought in. He had a broken arm too, and a bullet in his inside somewhere, and seemed very bad. Under Josh's instructions he too was put on the floor next to me, and so close that I was always afraid of his touching my wounded arm.

The Boer family did nothing but stare at us, but there was one little chap called Hans, about six years old, who was very good in fetching water for the trooper and me, and we spent our time in drinking water and vomiting most of the afternoon. My arm began to bleed again; there was no one to stop it for me. I began to feel very weak, and felt that I did not mind if I bled to death, more especially as I had quite settled that my arm was lost It was dark and raining when Dr. Hardy turned up. He had commandeered a spider with six mules and a Boer driver. He had also brought with him Reade, Colour-Sergeant Davies and some men. The first question I asked was as to how the day had gone, and it was a great joy to hear that we had turned them out of that hill, and that they had retired across the Buffalo. But what terrible losses! Colonel Gunning, Jack Pechell, Barnett, Taylor, and Hambro all killed, and many wounded, including Oliver Nugent, Boultbee, Johnson, Martin, General Symonds, and all his staff.

I will not attempt to describe what happened on the other side of the hill; how the general went straight at the hill with three battalions, and after a short but wonderfully accurate fire from our guns, carried it with frightful loss (over 250 killed and wounded); how our guns shelled our own troops by mistake, and killed many of our bravest and foremost men; and how we lost more than the other two regiments together, including five officers killed and seven wounded. All the details are well known.

If only this victory had been followed up, these terrible losses might have been less hard to bear, for a day which seems to me to have only been drawn in our favour would then have been one of the most decisive and important victories in the history of South Africa. But as it was, after the brilliant assault of Talana, the infantry soldier was deprived of his turn with rifle and sword-bayonet; the artillery, who were brought into position on the captured heights, were forbidden to fire at the mass of Boers, guns, and waggons, which were retiring in the open in great confusion within their range, while the cavalry and M.I. were being led in the opposite direction, to be made prisoners by 7000 Boers under General Joubert.

Trooper Masters and I were got into the cart somehow. Hardy put his coat on me, and a rug on the trooper. It was raining hard and very cold, and it was a five-mile drive to the farm on Talana, which the Boers had made into an ambulance hospital. The driver walked himself and drove the mules at a walk; he drove well, and did all he could to save us, but the road was bad, and we both felt it a great deal, groaning and vomiting at every bump of the cart. Crossing the *spruit*, where we saw the bodies of the poor maxim gun detachment, the cart nearly upset, and we cannoned into each other Hardy rode just in front, picking out the best road. It must have been about 10 p.m. when we got in, and a place was found on the floor for the two of us, side by side, in an outhouse.

There were three men also sleeping in the place, Irishmen of a low type, who had been commandeered, and who wore red cross badges, for they were by way of being hospital assistants. Their doctor told them to look after us. My feet were very cold; one of the men took off my boots and rubbed them, for which I was most grateful. The only other attendance we got was brandy and water, of which I was very glad too. There was a liberal supply of brandy, and I thought the "hospital assistants" did themselves pretty well. The night dragged on; it seemed to have no end. The hospital assistants turned in and had a snoring match. Poor Masters seemed to be dying, and kept asking for water, but I couldn't help him.

At last day came, and they said our ambulance carts would come for us soon, but no carts appeared to be coming. The place was full of men with red crosses on their arms, all loafers, who knew nothing of ambulance work, and who were there for their own safety. They ate all the food intended for the wounded. There were about sixty wounded

Boers, and a few English, among these Cape, of the 18th Hussars. Many of the slightly wounded Boers came in and looked at us. They shook their heads gravely, as if it was all up with us. Some came and talked to me; all were kind and sympathetic Our shrapnel seemed to have done terrible work among them, and we quite agreed that modern warfare was "not *ghut*" They kept leaving in large numbers with rifles, ponies, and waggons; and all seemed agreed that they did not intend to fight any more. The force we had met came from Vreiheid, Utrecht, and Krugersdorp, and were under Lucas Meyer, "the Lion of Vreiheid," about 4500 strong. They had crossed the Buffalo at de Jaeger's Drift, and occupied the Talana position after a long and quick night march.

Still the time dragged on, and we at the farm seemed to have been forgotten. The thought of being deserted, and the feeling that my arm wanted dressing, made me fretful and feverish. About 12 noon some of the Dundee Town Guard came up and found us. I told them how we stood, and one of them rode back for the ambulance. The Boers had nearly all cleared now except the badly wounded.

About one o'clock the ambulance turned up, and at last we got away. Hardy, who had turned up again, put Cape and me into the same waggon. The jolting was very bad, and I don't know how I should have stood it but for Cape holding my shoulder for me. We got into camp about 2 p.m. Cape and I were put into a hospital tent together; there were no beds or mattresses available, so many had been wounded. General Symonds was lying next to us, hit in the stomach. The ground was wet and muddy. Someone, however, got my valise and a rug for me, and I lay on that. The troops were out somewhere, and we could hear firing in the direction of Glencoe.

About 3 p.m. we had just got fairly settled, when from Impati ridge, about 4000 yards away, there was a bang, and we heard a shell whizzing over in our direction. It exploded near the stores in camp, about two hundred yards away. Another and another! They were shelling the camp. One struck the ground seventy yards from us, and sent the mud splashing all round our tent. It was the most unpleasant experience I had yet gone through. This bombardment came to an end after about twenty shells, but it left a very uneasy feeling. Why did our guns not answer?

The next day guns were heard again towards Glencoe; we got the rumours of the victory at Elandslaagte, and we heard that Sir George White was coming up, and with us was going to go for Joubert and that beastly Long Tom on the ridge. But soon the truth came out. General Yule was going to retire from Dundee, and was off *via* Helpmakaar, leaving us to our fate.

I lay in the camp for forty-eight hours in the tent with Cape. I had fever and a lot of pain, so I fear I must have been a nuisance to him. The army doctors were very busy; they never dressed my wound, or looked at it; the attendance was very bad, and we had to call for hours before we could get anyone to answer.

Under these circumstances I was very anxious to get to the civilian hospital in the Swedish Mission buildings in the town, where many of the worst cases were. I managed to work this, and at 2 p.m. on Sunday, October 22nd, was, with very great pain, transferred in a *dhoolie*. Now it seemed to me that the Boers had a special grudge against me, for only one shell was fired from the Impati ridge this day, and that landed within a hundred yards of my *dhoolie* while I was being carried halfway between the camp and the town.

It was an anxious moment as I heard the report and then the shell whirring over in my direction. The *dhoolie* bearers stopped short, and I expected they would drop the *dhoolie* and bolt. I caught hold of the top pole with my left hand, ready to break the fall. I shouted to them "*Chelo!*" (go on) and said the shells would never hit hospital "*log*" (people), but I was expecting another shell every moment, though none came.

The hospital I was taken to was originally intended for the wounded of the Town Guard, and was under Dr. Galbraith; after the battle, however, it became so full with wounded soldiers and Boers that it was put under an army doctor.

On reaching the hospital I was moved very scientifically into a most comfortable bed in the Swedish Mission buildings. This being the first time I had been under a roof or in a bed for a month, the luxury was the more appreciated. So what with this, and the kind attention of the doctor and his staff, I soon felt quite well again.

Soon after my arrival, the door opened and in walked a most attractive young lady—a nurse as I thought at the time. "By Jove," I said to myself, "you will have to watch it when you are getting better." However, to my relief, this turned out to be a married lady, none other than Mrs. Galbraith, who proved herself a heroine indeed that afternoon, and whose subsequent nursing and cheerfulness were such a help to all.

Soon after we had got settled down I heard yells and hooting, and the sound of a lot of horses coming down the street towards the hospital. "*Ce sont les Hollandais,*" I heard the Italian lady say, as she rushed to the door. I could not move myself to look, but I knew she was right, and that the Boers had come into the town.

"Well," I thought, "these are the chaps who have been threatening to shoot the first '*rooibatchi*' they see, or indeed any '*rooinek*.' These are the people who shell our hospital when the Red Cross flag is flying. How are these ignorant Boers going to deal with me?" I must confess I felt a bit uneasy, and had visions of Boers coming and pointing rifles at my head. It was not till afterwards, when they used to come in and sit on my bed filling my pipe for me, and showing me other attentions, that I learned that the Boers are as civilised as we are. (And I take this opportunity of saying that all the Boers I have met up till now, December 1900, have been kindness itself, and that their dealings with our wounded have been everything one could desire.)

Elated by their success, excited with drink, and under the impression that there were still some troops in Dundee, the Boers rode into the town, each with his rifle cocked, and ready to shoot the first British soldier he saw. Anyone will realise the risk of meeting men in such a mood—it was Mrs. Galbraith, while others hung back, who went out to meet them. She told them the English had left the town, that this was a hospital, and that it would be bad for the wounded to be disturbed.

It was a great relief to me when, after examining my arm, Dr. Galbraith, with his more up-to-date knowledge, told me that the amputation of my arm, which had been threatened, was not likely to be necessary.

After three weeks of comparatively good health—during which in spite of my arm I was able to write my diary—my temperature on November 13th went up to 105°, remaining there or thereabouts until November 20th. During this time I developed erysipelas, and could neither sleep nor breathe freely, being only half conscious. On the 30th some bone came out of the wound, I suddenly felt well again, and had a normal temperature. All through this crisis I was saved by Dr. and Mrs. Galbraith, of Dundee, who fought for me without resting.

There were at the Swedish Mission Hospital besides myself, Major Nugent, D.S.O., Lieut. Carbery, Sergeant-Major Burke, R.D.F., and about thirty men who had been wounded too badly to be moved with the remainder to Ladysmith—and I am sure there is not one of them who will ever forget the good work done by the Galbraiths.

Towards the middle of December I was coming to life again, and beginning to take an interest in what was going on; but what a time it was to come back to life! The siege of Ladysmith and the invasion of Natal had been shocks, but the worst time of all for us, was when we heard of Magersfontein, Stormberg, and Colenso. We only got the Boer versions, and only half credited them, still we knew we had been badly beaten all along the line; we could not hear what they were doing at home, or what the response of the nation would be. I for one, even in my weak state, swore to become a Frenchman, a Russian, anything but a Briton, if we did not see the war out, and I shall not easily forget the feeling of great relief when I did hear how the nation joined by the Colonies, the United Empire, was rising to the occasion.

Gradually we all began to get better, I shared a house with Nugent, and we used to listen to the guns, which we could hear distinctly at Ladysmith and Colenso, Some days the sound seemed to come from the east, and some days from the west, and on some it seemed to grow nearer and nearer. This change in the sound would cheer us up, leading us to picture successful flanking movements and general advances on Dundee. But the days dragged on and no good news ever reached us. At last, on Christmas Day, just as I was beginning to feel well enough to think about escaping to Greytown, the order came that the whole hospital was to be moved to Pretoria.

It was a sad day, December 31st, when the time came to part with the Galbraiths and Pastor Nauranius of the Swedish Mission, for, cut off as we had been from all friends and from all correspondence with our people at home, we had become great friends, and even situated as we had been, had had a happy time together.

PART 2

Departure From Dundee Hospital

On December 31st we started in the Boer ambulance train, a most perfect thing of its kind. The feeling of getting out after a long illness is always a great pleasure, and I remember feeling in high spirits as we steamed along through Glencoe towards Newcastle, with the country at its best. The line was guarded all the way to Pretoria, and at each culvert or bridge there was a small garrison, the defenders, as a rule, being housed in our bell tents, captured, no doubt, at Dundee.

Crowds came to look at us at each station; they were always friendly, and wanted to talk to us. But as we got nearer Pretoria my spirits went lower and lower, and New Year's Day found them very low indeed. How I hated the man on the train who on that morning said, "A happy New Year to you." How could we look forward to a happy new year when we were just entering on a period of captivity, the end of which seemed so far away? We arrived at Pretoria at 10 a.m. on New Year's Day. There was a large crowd at the station. Here the army doctor who had been in charge at Dundee, and all the orderlies, soldiers, and civilians were packed off to Delagoa Bay, and I said goodbye to Mr. Annis and Mr. Arnot, of Dundee, who had been so good to me.

We were now entirely in Dutch hands. The thirty men were taken to one hospital, while Nugent, Carbery, and I were taken to Burke's hospital. This hospital, for which the Boer officials took to themselves great credit, was run entirely by Mr. Burke, an Englishman and a resident of Pretoria. He was an extremely kind man; he saw that we had everything we required, and bore the whole expense himself.

There were in the hospital, when we arrived, Major Adie and Lieutenant Kentish, recovering from enteric, and twenty-three wounded Boers. Miss Lowry, the matron, was a trained English nurse; the others were Pretoria ladies, among them being daughters of Lucas Meyer and

BATTLE OF DUNDEE STORMING THE BOER POSTION ON TALANA HILL

of the late President Burgers. Though amateurs they were good nurses, and they fully carried out Lucas Meyer's injunction to his daughter, when he told her she was to treat the British just the same as the Boers. In fact I think some of them, possibly owing to the novelty of the thing, possibly owing to his more civilised ways, had a preference for nursing the British officer. Anyway, we were very good friends. Dr. Veale was our doctor.

The day after my arrival I had my arm X-rayed, and curiously enough in the dark-room I recognised the photographer as Tom Woolley-Dod, who had been an old friend and neighbour in Cheshire.

The Boer officials were most suspicious, and allowed no communication at first with the outside world. Instead of putting us on parole, and giving us a chance of convalescing, we were shut up all day in one room, not allowed to see the papers or any friends. Even when I had a tooth out the operation was performed by a dentist armed to his teeth with forceps and revolver, while the commandant and a *zarp* (policeman) armed with rifle and *bandolier*, were also present to see that I, no giant when in health, and at that time scarcely able to walk, did not try to escape.

I never had anything to say against the fighting Boer or his commandant, but the officials at Pretoria were mean and petty in the extreme, and it was only their great desire to appear civilised in the eyes of Europeans which made them treat us as well as they did. The meaning of "the word of honour of a gentleman" was quite unknown to them, so that they would not hear of my taking convalescent exercise on parole.

From January 12th we were allowed to see friends, *i.e.* one at a time from the officers, prisoners in the Model School. But the interview only lasted five minutes, with the Boer commandant listening to hear that no plans of escape were made and no news exchanged. The Boer commandant, who was a beast, might occasionally be detained by the offer of fruit or a cigar, and Dr. Gunning, the other warder, who was a good fellow, might be delayed by a discussion on philately, but at most these interviews never lasted a quarter-of-an-hour. The time went very slowly—day after day, nothing to do, no letters from home, and no news but bad news; so, after over six weeks without leaving my bedroom, I longed for a change of any kind, and as my wound had nearly stopped running, I, against the advice of those who knew the life, got transferred, on February 8th, to the Model School, where there were over ninety officers as prisoners.

On the whole, at first, I much preferred the life in the Model School. In hospital the food was better, but with only one window to look out of, and no chance of exercise, one had got very much bored. Here there was far more room, and there were lots of people to talk to. The building was a large oblong one with a path all round it. In front it had a verandah, and an iron railing between the path and the main road. At the back were a small playground, two baths, and a cookhouse. There were twelve *zarps* on guard all round the building. The bedrooms had nine of us in each, which was rather crowded; there were no shelves, nor anywhere to put one's belongings. Only one soldier servant was allowed to twenty officers. A bed, a mattress, one blanket, and a pillow were supplied.

At about 5.30 a.m., while all were in bed, the head-gaoler used to come round and count heads, to see that nobody had escaped in the night. About 6.15 I used to turn out to have my bath. The early mornings were lovely, so that even if one had to wait some time for one's bath, with a cup of coffee and a cigarette in the verandah, it was no hardship. When dressed I used to take about a mile walk before breakfast at 8.30. The meals were the worst part of the life. The room crowded and hot, overworked servants, a hundred of us at small tables, no table-cloth, unclean kitchen knives and forks, noise, bustle, dirty plates, indifferent food, and only water to drink. After breakfast one would smoke, talk and lounge in a deck chair in the verandah, and read books which could be got from the town library.

By noon it was quite hot At 1.30 we had another meal to face, after which I used to play patience, or lie on my bed reading, not infrequently allowing a *siesta* to pass away an hour. About four one would take a stroll round the estate, about one-ninth of a mile round. Tea at 4.30, a good square meal, after which some used to play rounders or quoits in the small playground at the back, while the majority took exercise, walking round and round the crowded court. At 7.30 p.m. dinner, a dirty piggery sort of meal, after which we were not allowed outside, and used to play cards, or talk or read, until about ten, when we turned in.

The hundred officers presented a weird sight, and it was no wonder that people passing on the opposite side of the road used to stop and have a good stare at us. One could imagine, when they stopped and talked to the *zarps*, that they were asking if we really were officers. Colonels, majors, subalterns, and magistrates, some no doubt, in better times, very particular as to their personal appearance, were to be seen with long hair and shaggy beards, dressed in all sorts of ready-made, badly-fitting, cheap Pretoria suitings. A scarf or muffler was more fashionable than a collar and tie, and a helmet usually gave a finishing touch to the get-up, for the authorities would not allow any hat which might help towards an escape.

Almost every regiment was represented. There were also a few civilians, magistrates and police, and a parson, the Rev. Adrian Hofmeyer. Some of them had sad stories to tell of the mistakes made at Stormberg, Colenso, Magersfontein, Tugela and Colesberg—some had been taken rescuing wounded men, and many had been wounded; some seemed quite happy and contented, whilst others showed signs of melancholia. It was indeed a despairing, hopeless kind of feeling, to know that this existence might go on for months, perhaps for years, and every keen soldier must have felt being out of the running.

I was joined here by my servant Faulkner, who when I was hit had been told to leave me, and had shared the fate of Colonel Moller's party. There had been much difficulty in getting hold of him, and it was only after a Cabinet Council meeting in the Volksraad that permission was given for him to be brought from the men's camp at Waterfall.

On my first Sunday I was much impressed with the service conducted by Adrian Hofmeyer; his extempore prayers and sermon were delivered with great feeling and eloquence. He had a robust voice, and used to play the organ and sing the first verse of the hymn to give us the tune, and then, having given us a start, he branched off into tunes of his own, so that with the farmers' bass of the majority, the part-singing of the few musical ones, and the fancy part-singing of old Hofmeyer, we kicked up a noise worthy of any cathedral. We used to finish up with the hymn for absent friends, as sung in Westminster Abbey, which left more than one damp eye, and a lump in many a throat.

The inhabitants seemed very anxious to have photographs of us, but when any Kodak or other photographing fiend turned up, the alarm was given and everyone turned his back on the camera. One day a closed cab, with the window-blinds down, drove up, and came to a halt close to where a lot of fellows were standing leaning over the railings. Suddenly a peep-hole opened in the window of the carriage, and it was seen that there was a camera inside. Everyone turned round, and stones were thrown at the cab, which galloped off, having, I hoped, failed in its object.

One afternoon after lunch, about the end of February, I was lying on my bed reading a novel. The heat was excessive and the book very dull; sleep was upon me, and I was just dozing off, when I heard the rush which always took place when letters arrived, but having been so often disappointed at not getting letters, I did not bother. I was half asleep, and seemed to hear my name being called. It went on in a monotonous way, getting louder and louder, till at last I was awake, and it dawned on me that there were letters for me and my name really was being called.

Over fifty letters came for me altogether, dating from Sept. 1899. I was indeed glad to have at last established communication with my people and many friends, and near as I had often been to them in my thoughts I was brought still nearer by this mail. We were sentimental in those days, and I was very much so that afternoon.

Our numbers increased as time went on. On February 25th there was a rush to the back door. More letters? No, it was six new prisoners. The prison door opened, and in walked Dr. Gunning, leading the way, with his pipe in his mouth, followed by six men, all of different regiments, bearded and burnt, in dirty torn khaki; evidently they had had a rough time of it. They all looked smart, workmanlike fellows. How was it, one wondered, that smart fellows like these kept on being taken, while we never heard of any corresponding captures on the other side?

These new arrivals looked puzzled at first at the sight of this wonderful collection of officers in odd clothes, and with beards and whiskers; but gradually friends recognised each other, and each of the new arrivals had a crowd round him, firing questions at him. What about Cronje? Kimberley? Ladysmith? and a hundred other queries. Most of these fellows seemed to know very little, for it is not the way in our army for subordinates to know too much. They are not like the wounded Boers who used to come into the hospital. Each of those Boers was a bit of a general himself; he knew what was going on all over South Africa, and would give intelligent accounts of many battles, with his own comments on the strategy and tactics of each side. Thus our numbers were constantly increased, and thus we used to gather news of how things were going.

But we had another source of information which was the greatest godsend to us. How Patterson, of the telegraph department, used to come over daily with the latest confidential wires to Kruger, and how the Miss Cullingworths, who had learned to signal with a flag, used to signal the news from the back of their house to our signalling officer,

A DASH FOR LIBERTY FOILED HEADING OFF GENERAL CRONJE AT THE MODDER RIVER, FEBRUARY 17TH

the worthy Captain Burrowes, is a story too well known for me to go into fully. From this source, from about February 22nd, good news began to come. The relief of Kimberley, the surrounding of Cronje, the successful advance at Peter's, the chaos at Boer headquarters,—all these were known to us and to Kruger alone, in Pretoria. Our spirits went up and the days seemed shorter.

Majuba Day was suitably celebrated at Paardeberg and on the Natal side, and it was also celebrated in Pretoria by the escape of Haldane, Le Messurier, and Brockie, for it was on that day that they were found to be missing. Many a time had I sat wondering how I could escape, and I was often so desperate that I would have attempted anything with a shade of a chance of success, but it had always seemed quite impossible. I could not conceive how these three had managed it I envied them and admired them, and no one could have been more astonished than I was when I heard what they had done.

On March 14th we saw Cullingworth and Patterson marching off to the front with rifle and *bandolier*. The Boers knew that we were getting the news, and suspecting these two, without being able to prove anything against them, sent them off on commando. We were getting too large a party for the Model School, and the authorities feared more escapes, so on March 16th we were moved to the place now known as the "Birdcage," which had been built to receive the Ladysmith garrison.

It was only at this time that we heard how Haldane and his party were still living under the floor at the Model School. The fact came out when others, proposing to escape in the same way (remaining underground when the rest were moved) magnanimously decided to forego their attempt in order that Haldane might have a better chance.

We were moved, beds, bag and baggage and all, through the town to our new abode, which was situated a mile outside to the north of the town. We drove up in cabs, escorted by all that were left in Pretoria in the shape of Burghers—the Boer "*landwehr*," consisting of boys too young to manage their ponies and rifles together, and of very old men. The building was a long low draughty corrugated iron barn, with only one partition. It had a few small windows high up, and only a mud floor. It was a place more suitable for cattle than men. There was no shade to be had, and the sanitary arrangements were disgraceful. There was a dense wire entanglement all round, at some distance from the barn.

Our first step on arrival was to draw up a strongly-worded protest, which was signed by every officer, and forwarded at once to the authorities. Shutting 130 of us up in such a barn was quite bad enough for my taste, but how had they intended to get the whole Ladysmith garrison into the same place!

Our Government had refused to consider any exchange of prisoners, a decision which, though one regretted it, one felt to be very sound. At this time we were very sanguine, the Boers seemed to be collapsing, and we did not expect to be shut up more than another month.

After a day or two in the Birdcage one began to see some advantages in it. Here we were high up, had grand air, and a fine view with beautiful sunsets. I bought a large Japanese umbrella tent under which we used to sit and read. Here naturalists had leisure to study the ways of snakes, salamanders, bugs, locusts and butterflies, and the botanist also had a limited field of research. There was a lot of rain about this time, making it damp muddy and uncomfortable inside the barn, with the result that there was a chorus of coughing and sneezing all day long, I, for one, owing to the draughts, never getting rid of my cold till I was released. It was a miserable place to feel seedy in; one could get no privacy, and one could not escape the whistling draughts that came through the badly-built building.

About March 25th the guard of *zarps* was exchanged for one of Hollanders, most inoffensive looking foreigners, clerks, shopkeepers and the like, whose larger numbers made up by quantity that which was lacking in quality. Opperman and Dr. Gunning were dismissed for having let three prisoners escape, and their place was taken by a Hollander grocer, who was a sensible sort of fellow and civil enough. He found Opperman's office full of back letters for us, which he delivered, and of unposted letters, which he posted.

Having read in one of our letters disparaging remarks on the martial appearance of his commando, and on the improbability of his men being able to hit a haystack, the new commandant started to drill his men, and sent them off to do a bit of musketry training with their old Martinis. They chose as a target a *kopje* at the back of our building, and all day long bullets came buzzing like locusts, flying harmlessly over our heads in the direction of Pretoria. Whether they learned to hit the *kopje*, or whether the people in the town protested, I do not know, but the musketry course came to an end after two days.

Their marksmanship was put to the test on April 5th when five of

The rush to Kimberley the 10th Hussars crossing Klip Drift

our number made a bid for freedom. At about 9.45 p.m., some clever electrician was to extinguish all the electric lights, inside and out. The lights did go out, and as they went out so did the *desperadoes*, each from a different door, and made straight for the wire entanglement Unfortunately, however, just as they started, something went wrong, and the electric lights flared up again, giving the whole thing away. Two or three shots were fired and the attempt failed. In the meantime the officers inside were in some anxiety. Some lay flat on the ground, and some put up hasty defences. I was in bed myself, so that this was my second experience during the war of being under fire in bed. Kentish, who was playing chess, said that one of the bullets came in and took the head off his queen!

April came to an end, and still the end of our captivity seemed no nearer. Perhaps we had been too sanguine. The advance seemed so slow to us, and the continued arrival of prisoners was not reassuring. A description of these latter days of April and the beginning of May, would be as depressing as the account of poor Dreyfus on his "*Ile du Diable.*" The "hope deferred," the absence of news, the discomfort and the depression, the disappointed ambitions and the want of health, all made the time drag very heavily.

In May, however, we began to get better news. The advance on Bloemfontein seemed to be going well, the Boers seemed to be wavering, but still we had this anxiety—should we be besieged in Pretoria, or carried off into the mountains of Zoutpansberg or Leydenburg? On the 13th Hofmeyer was released, and we all turned out to see him off. As he drove away we gave him quite an ovation, for we should miss him, especially his Sunday services, and his translations each evening of the *Volkstein*, a local paper which we were now allowed to take in.

On the queen's birthday we had, after some discussion, got leave to send a telegram from ourselves and from the men at Waterfall to Her Majesty—and to celebrate the occasion we were for the first time allowed port wine! It was bad fiery port wine. I only took one glass (in a mug) and had a mouth like blotting paper next morning—one would do a great deal for the queen! After drinking "the Queen" came "God save the Queen" which had been forbidden so long. We thundered it—every word, every letter, was sung with an emphasis and an impetus I had never heard before. A pent-up, stirring volume of loyalty, coming from 150 men. The room was barely big enough for 150 men, and it is a marvel to me how the roof stood such an explosion.

The Union Jack floated over Pretoria that day, for Haserick let loose a tame hawk with a Union Jack tied to its neck, and sent it hovering over the town.

On the 29th we had been hearing guns all day in the direction of Johannesburg. Rumours of our being moved kept us on tenterhooks all day.

The 6000 men at Waterfall, ten miles away, of whom we had never been able to get news, had, as we now heard, got out of hand on hearing the guns. The Boer authorities had tried to move them, but they had refused to move. Kruger had fled to Middelburg. Colonel Hunt warned the Boer authorities that if any men were shot the Boers would have to take serious consequences, and he offered to send officers to keep order, on condition they were not moved. It would have been a serious matter if 6000 men had broken loose and celebrated, perhaps with alcohol, this great occasion, in a town already in a state of chaos.

About 8.45 p.m. Hay, the American consul, and Lee Wood came in while we were at dinner. Hay received an ovation as he came in. They sat down and had a glass of port and a smoke. It very soon transpired that the British were expected in the town next morning. The town was upside down. Irish, Americans and foreigners who had fought for the Boers, were looting and drinking and taking their payment in kind. Oom Paul had fled for Holland, and Hay was practically governor of Pretoria. Then the Hollander commandant entered, and amid cheers said that he expected the British in the town next day. He appealed to us as soldiers, not to make it difficult for him to do his duty until the time came for us to change places with him. Colonel Hunt said we all thanked him for what he had done to improve our circumstances as far as he could.

We gave him three cheers—very hearty ones—for we were all ready to cheer anyone or anything. Then Colonel Hunt thanked Hay and Wood for all they had done for us, and we cheered them for all we were worth, singing "For he's a jolly good fellow." They each thanked us and were visibly pleased. Then came "God save the Queen." It was a record on the queen's birthday, but I think we just beat the record this time. We were sober enough, but drunk with joy and enthusiasm. I wish the good queen could have heard us. It was a great night. I shall never forget it. Twenty-five officers left for Waterfall that night to join the men.

Friday, June 1st.—Two days ago we were on the point of being free. The Boers were in a panic; if only they had been followed up we should be free. But something seems to have gone wrong; rumours of a reverse, French killed, and all sorts of such-like inventions; everyone walking about very despondent today. If Bobs does not hurry up they will move us all up country, which would break my heart. But he will be here soon.

Sunday, June 3rd,—This is a terrible long wait Botha, who is about the best man they have, has stayed the stampede, and collected 15000 Boers to face us. They are said to have taken up a position seven miles from here, and have sworn to die or win. They are cornered, or should be after this long wait, so they may make a stand; but the shells may alter their decision, which I think more likely. In any case it will probably be a lively time for us when the defeated rabble come our way.

Monday, June 4th.—This morning, at about 9 a.m., guns were heard quite close. We knew the Boers, 15000 strong, had taken up a position about six miles out, and it was said they had solemnly sworn to die or win. At 10 a. m. we saw a shell burst over the hill to the south, close to one of the forts. Then shrapnel after shrapnel was landed just over the fort and all along the crest line, about four miles away from us. Then some larger gun placed a lyddite close to the big fort, sending up an enormous column of red dust, and making a huge report. It was a grand sight. It went on all day, and we sat there in deck chairs watching.

We could see very few Boers about. About 3 p.m. we saw the balloon some fifteen miles off, I should think. Later in the afternoon the railway was shelled near the suburbs, and just before dark, away to the west, we saw clouds of dust, and what we took to be fleeing commandos. After such a day we all went to bed in excellent spirits. Our long depressing wait was very near its end, and we should now escape the terrible fate of being moved away to the east.

About 1 a.m. we were awakened by the commandant, who turned on the electric light and walked along the line of beds, saying, "Pack up, gentlemen; you have got to start at 3 p.m. and march six miles."

"Why?"

"I don't know why; those are my orders."

"Which direction?"

"To the railway, to the east."

Well, I knew what that meant at once, for I had expected the move for the last month, and many a very depressed hour had I spent thinking of the possibility of being carted about for six months in the cold—no food, no news, and every chance of being shot down. I lay in bed thinking what I should do; what we ought all to do. Some got up at once, and dressed quite ready to move, saying they were only going to move us out of range of the firing.

But Colonel Hunt luckily was not of that opinion, and nearly everyone felt what it meant. We knew nothing for certain, but we thought our people were only six miles off. Outside the Hollander guard had been trebled—about two hundred—and there were about twenty armed and mounted Boers. It was soon agreed that no one should move unless a rifle was pointed at his head. The Hollanders are only half-hearted, and the Boers don't act without leaders. So the commandant and sub-commandant, who were alone inside, and only armed with revolvers, were made prisoners. They were told that we refused to move, that they would have to shoot, and that if they did shoot, everyone of them would be hung by Bobs, who, we knew, was only seven miles off.

Well, the Hollander commandant was talked round, and fairly bluffed. He undertook not to move us, and to become a prisoner of the Boers if they insisted. He went out and had a talk with the Boer commandant; they had words, and the Boers galloped off to the town, calling him "a —— Hollander," and saying they would have to get a maxim. We had delayed the thing, anyway for a time, and the railway might be cut any time by French.

It was frightfully cold; I did not turn in again. Many went and hid in the roof, in ditches, and all sorts of places, where they were bound to be found. I got a bread knife and cut a hole in the rabbit wire, which was only a small part of the obstacle, and asked the Hollander sentry to look the other way if I tried to get out when the commando came. But there were so many of them that one was afraid of the other. He only hesitated and said he would see. We waited on till daylight, and no one came. We looked anxiously at the hills all round in hopes of seeing our troops on the hills, but could see nothing. We waited and watched anxiously, and thought we should have a day of suspense.

Tuesday, June 5th.—About 8 a.m. large bodies of men were visible to the west, about seven miles off, but it was impossible to say whether they were our men or Boers. Even if they were our men it was possible that we should be hustled off under their noses. About 9 a.m., two men in felt hats and khaki with a civilian galloped up. Even till they were a hundred yards off I feared they might be Boers. Then they took off their hats and waved them. There was a yell, and we all rushed through the gate. They were Marlborough and Winston Churchill, and we were free! We jolly soon had the Boer flag down, and the soldier servants, armed, on sentry over the Hollanders inside as prisoners. A Union Jack, made by one of our fellows for the great moment, was hoisted. Majendie and I tore down the hill into the town, running and yelling. It was a grand feeling being free again. When we got into the town we found British sentries over all the government buildings, Kruger's house, and all the banks, &c.

It would have been rather a shock to anyone accustomed to seeing the smart guardsman on sentry in Pall Mall to have seen him in the square at Pretoria, with his beard, dirty clothes, worn khaki, and battered helmet, with a toothbrush, spoon, or some such useful article taking the place in his helmet of the ornamental plume in his busby, a loaf of bread, a cooking-pot, and many other necessaries not laid down in the regulations as part of his equipment.

It was about 10.30 when we got into the town, and Bobs was not timed to arrive before two. So we looked round the place till then, watching the various troops coming in and posting sentries over the public-houses, banks, hotels, &c. They all looked most business-like and fit, sunburnt and covered with dirt and dust I lunched with Nugent, Colonel Hunt, and others, the first decent lunch for ages—clean table-cloths, glasses, plates, &c, all very much appreciated. We were waited on by one of our late guards, a German waiter!

By 2 p.m. all the prisoners of war were drawn up in the square, where we got a good view of the proceedings. I will not go into them, as the papers at home have no doubt given full details. It was a grand moment when the Union Jack went up, with Lord Roberts and Kitchener sitting on their horses at the salute. The troops marched past, not all of them, but quite enough to make an impression. They looked most serviceable, though some of them must have been very nearly done up. Though these fellows have had no fighting compared to the Natal troops, they have had very hard work, and the cold nights and short rations must have found out the invalids long ago.

I was jealous of the Mounted Infantry when I saw them, and I felt that the entry into Pretoria was quite incomplete without a Rifle regiment being there. But still the sense of being free again drowned all other feelings. The Woolley-Dods found me out, and have been putting me up since then. I have not time to go into raptures over their hospitality and kindness, and the joys of having a room to one's self and a hot bath, and lots of other comforts. They have been kindness itself.

On June 6th Lord Roberts saw all the released officers. We formed up in a long line in front of his house. Having lost all my uniform, I had to appear in flannels, with a muffler and a slouch hat. Lord Roberts had a word for everyone, and especially for those who had been captured on his side of the country, seeming to remember all the circumstances.

MOUNTED INFANTRY HALTING ON THE ROAD

PART 3

From Release, June 5th, 1900, to Rejoining Regiment, October 4th, 1900

Well, what now? Was I to go on? Was I well enough? Was it worthwhile after such a bad start? At this time it looked as if the war was about over, and I felt it was late in the day to "chip in." At the same time I was very keen to see a little more soldiering, so I made up my mind to join Colonel Alderson's Mounted Infantry if possible. This I could have managed easily enough by myself, but being reluctant to leave the men who were with me at Dundee, I decided to try and get them with me.

It was not till late on June 6th that the 3000 odd prisoners out at Waterfall, ten miles north of the town, were released. They, and the cavalry brigade which released them, were shelled by the Boers, and the released prisoners kept on arriving all that night in driblets in considerable disorder. Having run and walked the whole distance in their weak state, they arrived much exhausted. They had no rugs, no food, no shelter, and were altogether in a bad way. Still they were *free*, keen to go on with the war, and ready to undergo any hardships. There were about sixty men of my regiment, many of whom had been wounded at Talana. It was touching to see these poor chaps, mostly in rags, so pale and starved, so pleased to see their officers again, and though quite unfit, so keen for another chance.

But they got little encouragement The army in Pretoria was busy with its own work. It had anxieties on all sides. The supplying of 30,000 men by a long and threatened line of communication, the taking over of the towns of Johannesburg and Pretoria, and the continual fighting with the Boers who had rallied under Botha, meant that little attention could be paid to the prisoners of war. Thus it was for a week they were kept camped in the open on the race-course, short of food and clothing, and no rugs to keep out the extreme cold.

There seemed to be a feeling with some in Lord Roberts' army that the large number of prisoners of war was a disgrace, and that cases of surrendering had been unnecessarily frequent This feeling was, I think, to a certain extent shared at home. And yet, the number of our men taken prisoners was not excessive compared to that in former civilised wars, while it seemed not to be realised that the altered conditions of modern warfare make surrendering more excusable. Mistakes and inexperience were sometimes the cause of surrenders, but in the very great majority of cases it was simply "bad luck," and in no case that I know of was want of courage ever the cause. The feeling referred to did however exist, and one officer in a high position informed us that "if he had his way, the whole lot of us would be strung up."

A court of enquiry was held on each case of surrendering, and on June 10th I went before my court. When I had stated my case, and the circumstances under which I was taken, the president asked me "why I had not offered any resistance?" I answered that being under the Red Cross Flag, and only half conscious at the time, I was unable to offer resistance. This officer surrendered himself, with all his men, very shortly afterwards.

Of our sixty men, only about half were passed by the doctor as fit for service. Those who were fit were re-armed with the only weapons available. Martini Henry rifles from the Boer arsenal. The idea was to send them down country and employ them on the lines of communication, where they could refit and recoup. But in the meantime that sportsman De Wet was astride of the railway line, and communication was interrupted, so that we were kept hanging about doing nothing.

About this time I recovered my diary for 1899, which had been picked up by a Boer on our evacuated camping ground at Dundee, and kept by him as an interesting memento of the war. It had been carefully studied by the Boer Intelligence Department, and each reference to the Boers marked with a blue cross, the more important ones with several crosses.

On June 17th I was suddenly ordered to go with seven other infantry officers, in charge of over 300 dismounted troopers from various cavalry regiments, to reinforce the garrison at Klip River Bridge and Station, which were threatened. Discipline is never at its best among "details" on active service, so With cavalry details short of N.C.O:s, under infantry officers, it is small wonder that entraining took a long time, and that I found things different from what I was accustomed to.

Armed with Martinis and Lee Metford rifles and carbines, we reached Klip River, south of Pretoria, after a cold and wet three hours in cattle trucks, and were dumped down in the mud and pitch darkness with no idea of the lie of the land. If I learned nothing else that night I learned that the cavalry trooper is master of very strong language, and, as Kipling says, he is *"no plaster saint"*

No Boers came, and when daylight arrived we saw that the garrison, the Irish Rifles, had made splendid trenches. They must have thought our arrival a mixed blessing, for they could have held the place by themselves for days. We were joined here by Colonel Carleton, R.I.F., with the dismounted men of the M.I. Among them were the men who had been with me at Dundee, so I got transferred back to them. After two days, as no Boers came, we all left for Kroonstad, O.R.C.

There was at this time only a limited supply of rolling stock, and we travelled, eighteen officers, in a very dirty cattle truck. The train was drawn by a donkey engine, which had to pull up very frequently to boil water, often halting for twenty minutes at places most undesirable from a tactical point of view, and giving De Wet, who was in the neighbourhood, some excellent opportunities. Colonel Bullock, with another train-load of released prisoners, was just behind us. We arrived at Kroonstad early on June 22nd, after thirty-six hours in the train.

Soon after our arrival we heard guns, and got the news that Colonel Bullock's train had been held up by De Wet at Honing Spruit, fifteen miles off. About 7 a.m. the Boers, 1000 strong, with three guns, surrounded Colonel Bullock with his 400 released prisoners, and on his refusing, as he had done once before at Colenso, to surrender, the Boers, well out of range themselves, opened a heavy fire from all directions, which fire they kept up till 1 p.m., when a relieving force arrived from Kroonstad. There was no cover to be had.

The Boers were bursting shrapnel with great accuracy from one of our guns taken at Sanna's Post, and our men had to lie flat without even firing, because they found that they could not, with their obsolete Martinis, make the Boers "lie down," whilst each shot they fired made a cloud of smoke which drew a hail of bullets. They did not, however, intend to be taken prisoners again, and though called on several times to surrender, stood their ground well until relieved. Poor Hobbs, of the West York, and five men were killed; one officer and seventeen men wounded. Of the detachment of thirty K.R.R. under Sergeant Bennewith, two were killed and one wounded.

We were very glad indeed to get to Kroonstad, which was at that time the most advanced base for Ordnance, Army Service Corps, and Remounts. We were tired of being shifted about from place to place, a ragged untidy mob, with little resemblance to soldiers, many men without boots or uniform, others carrying striped *Kaffir* blankets and bundles over their shoulders like tramps, and all armed with obsolete Martinis. We were a good "side show" for a war correspondent to describe, but the prospect of getting re-armed and re-equipped cheered everyone up, and with the improved scale of rations the men got visibly better.

At Kroonstad we found every variety of soldier, Regulars, Yeomanry, A. and S. Highlanders' Militia, C.I.V., Artillery Volunteers, Canadians, Australians, New Zealanders, and S. African Colonials. There was a rush for everything, and the huge packing cases which kept coming up from the coast, as fast as a single line and limited rolling stock could bring them, were very soon emptied. Lord Kitchener was on the spot to put things straight

In the general scramble of refitting, I was very successful, and by July 1st had my twenty-two men completely fitted out in everything, and had secured twenty-five good cobs with saddles, etc., complete. But the result of this keenness was, that instead of being sent up to join Colonel Alderson and General Hutton as I had hoped, we, being the first ready, were packed off with Grouchy and twenty-five men Leicester M.I. to Vredefort Road to do duty on lines of communication. We got orders at 1 p.m. to start at once. By 3 p.m. we had entrained horses and men. With the help of a donkey-engine (much riddled with bullets) after several stops to boil water, and after pushing it ourselves op a gradient which it could not negotiate, we eventually reached Vredefort Road (fifty miles) at 11 p.m.

I was in some ways disappointed at not getting to the Mounted Infantry under General Hutton, who were about to continue the big advance against Botha to the east—but perhaps we were hardly fit yet for such work, and were all the better for the chance we got of recouping at Vredefort.

Colonel U. Roche, whom I had known in India, was in command of the Vredefort garrison, which consisted of three Companies of

South Wales Borderers, two guns 60th F.B.R.A,, and our fifty M.I. He gave me the best breakfast I had had for a very long time—porridge, eggs and bacon, fresh milk, and batter and eggs. It may seem trivial to mention this, but after being deprived of these things for so long this breakfast was a great event for me.

We were soon quite reconciled to our new job, and settled down at once, rigging up shelters with railway waggon tarpaulins and corrugated iron, It was a great thing to feel that one had at last got a job, after such a long period of inactivity. The order and excellent arrangements of the S.W. Borderers, with their well turned out men, clean camp, field oven, etc., were a great contrast to the recent experience of chaos in camps of "details."

It is a terrible thing to become a "detail" Whether officer or man, a "detail," once separated from his corps, is "nobody's dog," and he has nobody to take any interest in him, beyond getting as much dirty work out of him as possible. At this period of the war, once separated from his regiment, a man had the greatest difficulty in getting back to it, and almost every garrison had its quota of grumbling "details."

It was not long before we had our horses out and were exploring the country. A grand ride it was, that first ride, as I cantered or trippled in the keen morning air of the open *veldt*, breathing in health and spirits at every breath. What a glorious feeling it gave of being really free at last And with returning health a great keenness came over me. The war-worn used to smile at this keenness. Almost every morning I used to take what men were available, and, starting long before dawn, ride out to some good point of observation five to nine miles off, arriving there as the sun rose, in the hopes of getting in touch with the Boers. Often we saw nothing, but occasionally had better luck, and before very long we had collected two horses per man and as much transport as we needed in the shape of Cape carts. We had also a few prisoners.

As a full account of the many raids and ambushes we made during our stay at Vredefort would weary the most patient, I will not describe them.

On June 25th General Sir H, Chermside, who was commanding the line of communication, passing through in his armoured train, sent for me and congratulated us on good work done.

About this time De Wet, having crossed the line with 4000 men, was run to ground by Generals Ridley and Broadwood at Parys on the Vaal, On the other side of the Vaal were Lord Methuen and Lord Kitchener, and the capture of De Wet was looked upon as a certainty, if only the troops, which were being hurried up from the scene of Prinsloos surrender, could come up in time.

I rode more than once with confidential despatches from Pretoria to General Ridley, and had a good look at the positions. General Ridley was sanguine, and said if I came out in about six days I should probably see the end of it. Later General Hart passed through Vredefort with troops, hurrying to help in completing the circle round De Wet. I asked him if he could not take me and my twenty men, and he said he would ask General Chermside; his last words to me as the train left were—"All right, I won't forget you."

A few days later guns were heard at daybreak, and it became known that De Wet had in the night made a new drift across the Vaal and again escaped. The Boers seemed to cross the railway line and blow it up whenever they wanted to, and the patrols we had to send out each night were quite unable to prevent it, though they did once succeed in shooting a horse and stopping one attempt

In August, owing to the rheumatism which the cold weather had given me in my wounded arm, I left for Cape Town on the recommendation of the Medical Officer. I was extremely sorry to say goodbye to Sergt. Hill, Farr.-Sergt. Kennedy, and the men who had been with me so long and who had done so well, but I promised them, if I did not go home, that I would get back to the battalion, and get them back to it, if possible.

On August 19th I left Vredefort with Faulkner, sorry to part with my men and many other friends, but in high spirits at the idea of getting home, or getting back to the regiment with Buller. We made the journey to Bloemfontein in open coal-trucks; the days were lovely, and one did not travel at any great pace, so that it was a pleasant enough ride, and one got a good view of the country.

After a short stay at Bloemfontein, we left at 10 a.m. on August 2 1st in the ordinary fast mail train; a most comfortable saloon taking the place of the coal-truck

From here onwards there seemed to be perfect peace in the country; and making the ordinary peace-time journey, with halts for meals at the restaurants, we travelled on without incident, and reached Cape Town on the morning of August 23rd, Ending the rainy season in full swing, and the country a wonderful green, most refreshing after the dry *veldt* upcountry.

At Capetown I reported to the P.M.O., and was sent to the Claremont Convalescent Home, where sick officers were boarded and lodged free of expense. The place was full of convalescent officers, all trying to get home.

Finding that I should have to stay three weeks at this Home before I could even get a medical board, I applied to be sent to duty at once, and calling on Colonel Cooper, of the O.C. Troops, at the castle, I got an order to report myself at the Camp at Green Point, and to join my regiment the next opportunity. But I was kept three weeks at Green Point Camp, and it was not until September 16th that I embarked for Durban. This long delay was irritating, more especially as my regiment was seeing interesting service at the time under Buller. However, I found many old friends at Capetown, Wynberg, and Symon's Town, besides other army friends.

Having been reported in some Cape paper as killed at Talana, more than one old acquaintance came up and said, "Hello! I thought you were dead." The Kenilworth races were going on just as before, and many of the ponies running three years ago were still competing there, among them a famous old pony called "The Wake," formerly my property, and now fifteen years old.

I paid a short visit to Admiralty House at Symon's Town, during which the news arrived of Kruger's departure. A lovely drive round Table Mountain, dinners at the Mount Nelson Hotel, theatres, shopping, etc., besides an occasional court-martial on guard over Boer prisoners, and the time soon went, so that I sailed in the *Englishman* on September 17th all the better for my short return to civilization.

We left Table Bay at the same time as the s.s. *Kildonan Castle*, full of invalids for home, and it was perhaps a little tantalizing to see this fine mail-boat, 10,000 tons heading homewards, while we, on our cattle-boat 4000 tons left in the opposite direction, heading further away from home. We had on board 500 men, mostly young Irish soldiers, just out from home. I did adjutant to this lot as far as Maritzburg, where we arrived on September 21st These men are probably excellent soldiers by now, but they were very raw material then, and I was glad to get away.

Escaping being commandeered as a "detail" at Maritzburg, I stayed there only one night. I dined with the governor, Sir W. Hely-Hutchinson, so that I had an opportunity of telling him what good work Dr. Galbraith had done at Dundee.

At Newcastle, which was at that time a great trap for "details," I got stuck for two days. There were many here who had been trying for weeks to get back to their regiments, so that things looked bad for a bit. However, I met many friends here, and through one of them a wire came direct from General Lord Dundonald at Lydenburg applying for me.

I got to Pretoria on September 28th, after an interesting journey over the ground I knew so well. The country was in a very unsettled state, and we were several times delayed, owing to the line having been tampered with. In Pretoria there was almost a famine, the Grand Hotel, where I stayed with Salmon, being unable to supply milk, butter, eggs, jam, matches, or indeed anything but rations. There was the usual crowd of waiters, there were clean table-cloths and well-laid tables, but there was very little to eat.

My journey from Vredefort to my regiment had been circuitous and extremely slow; many obstacles had to be overcome. However, from Pretoria to Lydenburg, I did what was at the time a record. After securing three good ponies, saddles, stores, etc., I had the good fortune to foregather with Colonel Birdwood on Lord Dundonald's staff, who was returned, recovering from his wound.

We left Pretoria together, thirty-six hours after my arrival, in a special train with our horses and stores complete, and leaving a crowd of disappointed would-be travellers on the platform at Pretoria, we ran quickly through to Machadodorp without being sniped at, a thing unusual on this line; then, making double marches, we arrived at Lydenburg just as General Buller was returning there from Sabie's River, on October 4th.

Thus at last, after endless scheming and worrying, I had succeeded in getting back to the regiment I found the men of the battalion, with arms piled and accoutrements taken off, having their dinners and resting after a hard march. I pushed on, nodding to many a familiar face, past the grandest battalion of veterans I had seen during all my wanderings, to where the family circle of officers was, with Colonel Campbell sitting in the middle.

Back at last, and no longer a "detail," I was perfectly contented.

Part 4

October 9th, 1900, to February 1st, 1901

When I was last with the battalion, our Mounted Infantry formed part of the 1st Batt. K.R.R. But on arriving at Lydenburg I found that with three other companies of M.I. (the Leicesters, Liverpools and Manchesters) they were now known as the "4th Division M.I." and were quite separate from the battalion.

At first Colonel Campbell did not advise me to go to the Mounted Infantry, but seeing that I was so keen on it, and had brought three ponies with me, he consented to my going, so on October 5th I rejoined my old company under Scratchley.

Many changes had taken place in the Company since it started from Maritzburg under Northey. Talana, the siege of Ladysmith, and the subsequent advance under Buller, had made many gaps, which had been filled up by new men. Still, there were many left, such as Colour-Sergt. Rowat, Sergt. Ross, "old Shirley," and others who had been right through and never missed a day, and I was indeed glad to rejoin this company, which I had seen formed at Cape Town over four years before, and which *esprit-de-corps* made me think the best thing of its kind in the country.

After their two months and a half continuous trekking, all ranks had had enough for the time being. They returned to Lydenburg pretty sick of it. Everyone wanted to hear that the war was over, but I am afraid I had not much good news to give, for though there were rumours of Lord Roberts and General Buller going home, and though the advance to the east as far as Komati Poort was most successful, yet my own experience was that wherever I had been on the railway there seemed to be some local commando threatening the line, and boasting that it could go on fighting for years.

I was introduced to Lord Dundonald, and had the opportunity of thanking him for helping me to get up to Lydenburg. Unfortunately I did not serve under him for long. On October 6th he, with General Buller and many others, left Lydenburg for home. The departure of General Buller was a memorable scene, and the enthusiasm of his splendid army, when it said goodbye to him, was a proof to me, an outsider, of what those who knew him best, thought of him.

Scratchley had besides me two other subalterns, Lynes and Johnson, both officers of "tried valour." We four messed together in a very humble way, crouching under a tarpaulin, and drinking nothing at meals but ration tea and coffee. The small amount of stores, such as milk, butter, quaker-oats, and jam, which I had been able to bring up with me, were acceptable, but did not go far.

For a day or two after my arrival there was much speculation as to what would happen next. However, all doubt was removed on October 8th, when we heard that half the troops under General W, Kitchener were to remain and garrison Lydenburg, while the other half under General Lyttleton were to march direct to Middleburg, seven marches south-west of Lydenburg, on the Pretoria-Delagoa railway line.

Our company was to go with General Lyttleton, whose force consisted of K.R.R., Gordons, Leicesters, Inniskilling Fusiliers, 18th Hussars, one Battery R.F.A., one 5-inch gun and one pom-pom. Our route took us through some of the most mountainous country in the Transvaal, and there were plenty of Boers.

On October 9th we left Lydenburg. Our horses had been having hard work on short rations, and there was as yet very little grazing to be had, so that they were in poor condition. We were still, however, able to produce 80 mounted men out of 115. After three marches through a desperate country, a country very different from the O.R.C., we reached Dulstroom on October 11th. Had the Boers offered any serious resistance we must have had many casualties, but as it was, they contented themselves with sniping, and there were only one or two hit each day.

The column left Dulstroom early on the morning of October 12th, our 1st Battalion and two guns doing rear guard under Colonel Campbell, with our company as its mounted screen. We went out at daybreak two miles beyond the camp, taking up positions in an arc, facing the rear, Lynes to the left, my section in the centre, and Johnstone on the right, with the 4th section in support under Scratchley.

Our extended line soon came under a sniping fire from several directions, while Lynes on my left was also busy. We had to hang on till the baggage was well away, and our infantry battalion had retired beyond the village of Dulstroom. We were to retire by sections, Lynes' section first.

After a long wait, with occasional shots coming pretty close, the time came for us to retire, which we were in the act of doing, when I saw that Bugler Douglas, who had been sent over to me with a message, had got badly bogged. Telling my section where to go to, I went back with Sergt. Rowat to try and help him out. But it was a bad place, and the horse was exhausted. The stupid Argentine brute refused to make an effort, and sank deeper and deeper. A few Boers at about 500 yards had got our range, and were getting unpleasantly near, so we packed Douglas off on foot, and only stayed long enough ourselves to destroy the horse and saddle before the Boers could get them. Poor Douglas had a long run—he was picked up by Scratchley, who with some difficulty got him to the rear unhit but rather agitated.

When we had retired to the next position, Johnstone's section, well opened out, cantered quietly back, bullets striking the ground all round them.

The Boers, from 50 to 150 strong, kept pushing on as we retired, and from the high hill which overlooks the village of Dulstroom, they began to make things unpleasant for us. However, Colonel Campbell backed us up from the rear with his guns, and thus considerably eased the pressure. After one or two more retirements under a sniping fire, we eventually shook the Boers off, and by 12 noon there were very few to be seen. I have been in a good many rear guard fights since then, but never in one where men were better handled. It was a difficult country, and we were outnumbered, and it was due to Scratchley's good management that we did not lose a lot of men that day.

Our advance guard had bumped up against Ben Viljoen. As the advanced troops came down the steep hill near Witklip (ten miles beyond Dulstroom), and debouched into a kind of amphitheatre, they came under fire from a Boer pom-pom and Mausers. The 18th Hussars and Liverpool M.I. had one or two men hit.

The hills had to be cleared of these Boers. This was done by the Gordons and Inniskilling Fusiliers, who, well covered by the artillery, only lost two killed and six wounded. We, the rear guard, got into camp late that night in the dark, in a drenching thunderstorm. We made no attempt at comfort, and lay down as we were, with an early rise before us, and every likelihood of a fight with Botha and Viljoen.

October 13th, 1900.—To the right of the road we had to follow, and about three miles on, there were three *kopjes*, which it was probable the enemy would hold to oppose our advance. The two M.I. companies were detailed to seize these *kopjes*, and everything was made clear to us beforehand.

About 3.30 a.m. it was raining hard. We turned out of our wet blankets, fed somehow, and saddled-up. As day was breaking, about 5 a.m., we launched out, and supporting each other in waves, took each of the three kopjes in succession at a canter. The first two were unoccupied; the third was held by a Boer picquet, which the Liverpool Company completely surprised, taking the picquet and opening a heavy fire, which compelled a larger party of Boers beyond to retire. It was a smart move, smartly carried out, and greatly simplified the march of the column. By 9 a.m. the column had passed, and we pushed on, keeping on the right flank. There was shooting at long distances all this day, but no damage done, the Boers making no real attack.

We passed through several beautiful farms, better farms than any I had seen in the O.R.C. Every one of them had a white flag up, though we had been sniped at from the same farms five minutes before, and we often found the sniper's lair still warm. Crowds of womenfolk used to come out to meet us, protesting that their husbands, brothers, or sons were dead, or had not been seen for months, and denying having seen any Boers that day. In those days we never touched an occupied farm, and used to pay well for poultry, eggs, pigs, or anything we took. Occasionally we were shot at from the farm when we had left it We got into camp about 6 p.m., and Scratchley read an order complimenting the company on good work in the rear guard fight of the 12th.

On the 14th we got out of the mountainous country, and the 18th Hussars under Colonel Knox, with our company in support, spreading well out and covering a large front, captured some Boers and some horses, and large quantities of cattle and sheep. We camped about twelve miles from Middelburg, near Elandslaagte, where we had a lovely bathe and swim. Next day, the 15th, we arrived at Middelburg. We had met with little of the expected opposition, but this I have found generally is the case when the Boers see a large force in good hands. To me, with the interest of seeing a new country, and soldiering with so many old friends, it was a most enjoyable trek.

Arrived at Middelburg, our one idea was to rest, recoup, and re-fit, and for a few days the troops, men and horses, lived in peace, and began to get re-fitted with stores and remounts from Pretoria. On October 17th Scratchley went home, and I took over the command of the company.

We did not rest long. On both sides of the line there were active commandos, each about 250 strong. This was before the trying times of night attacks by large commandos under Ben Viljoen and Louis Botha, but it was nevertheless a most trying time for the mounted troops. The line was continually threatened. Small patrols were frequently in difficulties. Raids on the cattle or horses grazing beyond the camp were of daily occurrence. We lived in momentary expectation of the order, "Saddle-up." Many a time we did saddle-up, and turned out in shirt sleeves at a gallop, but however quick we might be we were never quick enough.

More than once, after a patrol had got into trouble, and returned with the loss of men killed, wounded, or taken prisoners, a column went out to punish the offenders, but invariably with the same result. The column would march out ten to twenty miles, driving before it any Boers seen. It would camp that night at some farm where the commando had been, and after stripping it of all wood, grain, vegetables, poultry, pigs, and furniture, would return next day. Our return was always followed up boldly by the Boers, and many a lesson in rear guard fighting they gave us.

At daybreak single Boers would be visible on the distant heights round us, watching our movements. When it became evident that we were going back to the line Boers sprang out of the earth, and very shortly afterwards each Boer, as seemed to him best, was galloping, stalking, shooting, or working round our rear guard. With ever increasing numbers and ever increasing boldness they would follow the column right up to within the outposts of Middelburg, and we considered ourselves lucky if we got back to Middelburg without having half-a-dozen men hit in this unsatisfactory manner. Thus it was no wonder that we failed to agree with the home papers when they insisted that the war was over. From a German strategist's point of view it may have been over, but to me, from my subaltern's point of view, the end seemed a depressingly long way off.

It was on one of these expeditions, on October 30th, that the 18th

Hussars, whom the general spoke of as "the best Mounted Infantry in the country" first used the rifle instead of the carbine. They were the first cavalry regiment to adopt the rifle, and I well remember the confidence they showed in the new weapon, thrusting ahead, dismounting and shooting.

On October 24th our 1st Battalion went up to Pretoria to help to represent the Natal troops in Lord Roberts' farewell Review. A splendid battalion they were, with veterans from India and Egypt, representatives of Talana, Ladysmith, Spion Kop, Tugela, and many other engagements. It was Freddy Roberts' old battalion, and they and the chief remembered this as they marched past him.

Soon after this the sad news of the death of Prince Christian Victor reached us, and the battalion again went to Pretoria to take part in his funeral. Many a man, as he saluted the prince for the last time, remembered him in India, and recalled the kindly interest he had always taken in his men. We all felt that we had suffered a loss most sad among our many sad losses in the war.

On November 6th my company was split up, thirty men under Johnstone going to Pan, twenty-five under Lynes to Whitbank, while I with the remainder, about sixty, moved to Olifants River, twelve miles west of Middelburg. At Olifants River, we, with sixty men, relieved Major Von Donop, R.A., with two companies of M.I., the authorities evidently considering one rifleman equivalent to three other men!

Our duty was to watch about six miles of railway in each direction. There was an important bridge there, and a garrison of four guns 83rd R.F.A., and three Companies K.O.S.B., to defend it There were many "enterprising Burghers" who kept us well occupied from the first. From my tent, high up, about 300 feet above the railway, I had a grand view of the country all round, and with a powerful telescope on a tripod at the door I could watch the movements of the small parties of Boers which were always to be seen on the skyline about five miles away. They could do nothing without being seen from our camp, but at the same time they were able to watch all our movements.

The chief danger was to our picquets along the line when they went out to their posts at daybreak, but we had the good fortune to have no casualties during our time, and only one train was blown up. This, compared to the luck of other sections along the line in these troubled times, was a good record.

Troubled times they were. Each day the Boers seemed to get bolder, and to collect in larger numbers. Each day guns were heard booming, sometimes at Balmoral, sometimes at Middelburg, sometimes at both places at once; and yet the papers kept saying the war was over.

On November 19th thirty Boers, under Commandant Piet Trichard, attacked seven of my men stationed three-and-a-half miles off in the direction of Middelburg. I had an exciting view of the whole thing. With Major Haig, K.O.S.B., and Major Guthrie-Smith, R.A., I had been watching these thirty Boers for some time from my tent. The range was taken, and found to be 9000 yards. I sent one man to warn the picquet of the presence of these Boers, but did not saddle-up the rest of the company, as they had already had a long day. For some time we watched the Boers collected under a tree, then they mounted and seemed to be riding off in a direction away from the picquet. Suddenly, however, I saw the whole lot scatter and swoop down towards the picquet I shouted to my men in camp to saddle-up, and watched through my glasses for all I was worth. The picquets' orders were, in case of attack, to retire fighting.

There were two miles between the picquet and the Boers, who covered the distance in no time. I heard heavy firing, saw two of the pig-headed Argentines refusing to be led to their men, saw the Boers, who were getting nearer every second, dismount,—and, leaving their horses, rush up, crouching and shooting. I feared all sorts of mishaps. The last thing I saw before galloping off was Boers, dismounted and extended, shooting at our men, only five of whom I could see falling back. We galloped down, and the guns too galloped down and opened fire very smartly, but the three miles and a half over rocky ground gave them time to get away, so we arrived on the spot only in time to save the railway. The delay of our picquet in getting away had been due to one of our "young hands" and the perverseness of his Argentine horse.

On November 25th we received a valuable reinforcement, Sergt. Hill and his twenty men having at last succeeded in getting away from the Free State.

If ever there was a "handy man" it was my servant, Faulkner. Very soon after we got to Olifants River he had fitted me out a comfortable home, and had furnished my tent with table, chairs, and a bed. He started a farm with good laying hens, ducks, geese, and a turkey to be fattened up for Christmas, He got milk, vegetables and fruit from the neighbouring farms; produced a stove, and catered and cooked for me, always remembering that I had lost most of my teeth. Besides all this, he was a bit of a rough-rider, and used to bring in wild colts, which in a few days he had broken and trained to perfect manners.

The climate and seasons of South Africa have always been a puzzle to me. These months, November to January, produced the wildest of winter storms, intense cold, with terrible thunder and lightning, sudden blizzards of wind and hail and deluges of rain, with intervals of most perfect summer weather or tropical heat, when one groaned at the heat and the flies.

Olifants River was a beautiful place, and its farms, orchards, and flowers, its clear streams, and the new green of the *veldt* were at their best at this season. When I had leisure I used to go down to bathe or fish in the river, or sit on its banks and forget for a time that there was a war going on, watching the kingfishers and sunbirds, the red finches and the long-tailed "*sakaboulas*," all in full plumage.

In December two expeditions were sent out to the north, to co-operate with columns under Generals Paget and Plumer against Ben Viljoen and Thais Pretorius, who had about 2000 men in the bush country round the Wilge River. The first of these was under Colonel Carleton (1st Leicesters) and the second under Colonel Campbell. On both occasions we found an escort of twenty-five men to the pom-pom under Captain Poole, R.A. We cleared the country, which we found full of well-stocked farms. We captured many waggons, a few Boers and cattle, but did little damage to the commando, which slipped away further north.

About December 20th there was fever in the air, and ten of my men and myself were laid up, but only for a short time. On Christmas Day most of them were able to enjoy the geese which we had been fattening up for the occasion, as also the beer and plum puddings which our battalion had sent us from Middelburg, while I was sufficiently recovered to make a short speech according to custom:

> In wishing you all a happy Christmas, (I said), I am glad of an opportunity of saying a few words. It is a long time now since we left India for this country, but I well remember how some of you then, wrote up in the Barrack rooms at Jullunder, 'Roll on Kruger's doom.' I well remember Christmas day, 1896, on the *Warren Hastings*—and those of you who are bad sailors well remember too—how the ship ' rolled on' right enough. Kruger's doom was 'rolling on' too, but we thought more about the ship then. Well, men, Kruger's doom has 'rolled on,' and our regiment has had a good share in passing Oom Paul along. One

man who has come well out of the war is the British soldier, and conspicuous amongst British soldiers have been the men of the King's Royal Rifles; so that you being picked men from the K.R.R., may hold your heads high—as high as the C.I.V. indeed.

What makes a good regiment? It is that good comradeship which exists amongst all ranks. It is the feeling which men have that they are responsible for the safety of men they are fond of, and responsible too for the honour of the regiment to which they are proud to belong. It is the devotion to duty and sense of honour which form part of the faith of every rifleman. Let us hope that, should we find ourselves at any time in a position of difficulty, the devotion to duty may find us prepared, and the sense of honour may see us through the difficulty, whether dead or alive, with increased honour to ourselves and increased honour to the regiment.

It was not a bad Christmas,—far better than most of us had had the year before.

People at home, who still thought the war was over, were shortly to have their eyes opened to the fact that we had not even yet reached the stage of guerilla warfare. Louis Botha had collected in the Bethel-Ermelo-Carolina district a commando of 2000. Ben Viljoen to the north of the line had another 2000. De la Rey and Beyers each had strong commandos, able to concentrate in one night. De Wet had 2000 good men, and was making good use of them in the Free State. All these commandos were fully organised, with guns, horses, and supplies, and were under the best Boer leaders. Besides these, there was some small commando to be watched at almost every station along the line, and there were rumours of coming trouble in Cape Colony.

The Boers changed their tactics. They had hardly been known to attack before, but they now commenced a series of most gallant, and in some cases successful, night-attacks. In our district, Belfast, Balmoral, Machadodorp, and Helvetia had all been attacked, and in some cases successfully. Still, we remained on the defensive The great move, which we all felt sure was being hatched at Pretoria, was not yet ready.

To meet this change in the Boer tactics, the garrisons all looked to their defences. They improved their *sangars*, making them all enclosed works, they dug new trenches and, collecting every available yard of barbed wire, put obstacles round their works. Garrisons, often short-handed, had to double their sentries, and, though *Kaffirs* and even dogs were called in to relieve the strain, still the work was hard, and it was a life of suspense. Each post along the line had its rumours of intended attacks, and its fits of "the jumps," which varied with the imagination of its Intelligence Department, or the nerves of its commanding officer.

In our station we had many reports that an attack on our bridge was coming. Our positions were rather extended for our numbers, so we slept with one ear awake. We daily added to the strength of our position, and by January we were ready for all comers, and rather hoped they would come. On January 1st Johnstone, who had been at Pan, a favourite haunt of the Boers, left to join the I. Lt. Horse, and his place was taken by Reade.

About the middle of January Botha collected 4000 men near Ermelo, and was reported to be going to invade Natal. This drew most of the Boers away from our neighbourhood, so that we were able to hold sports. Some of our detachment at Whitbank came over, and with them, the field and horse gunners, and the infantry we got fair entries for the events, which included races, foot and mounted, jumping, potato-race, bare-backed Lloyd Lindsays, and a tug of war between our men and the gunners. The local farmers and their families, and those of the garrison who could get away, made quite a crowd of spectators.

The contrast between the big gunners on their large draught horses and our smaller men on their cobs, when they stepped into the arena for the tug of war, amused the lookers-on, who shouted to our men to take care that they did not get pulled outside the picquets as there were Boers about. But the event proved a triumph of mind over matter, for our men, pulling hand-over-hand, and their cobs planting their fore-feet in the ground, soon pulled the R.A. and then R.H.A. (who tried to walk away with the rope) over the line. This most successful day was brought to a close by a distribution of prizes—Mrs. Bourhill, the wife of a leading *burgher* farmer, giving them to the successful competitors in most approved style.

In the small hours of the morning of January 23rd a cipher message was received, which proved to be that the commander-in-chief was coming down from Pretoria that day to see General Lyttleton at Middelburg, and that we were to take extra precautions along the line. I accordingly sent a sergeant and eight extra men to the west which direction was less exposed, and started myself at daybreak, with every available man to the east, in the direction of Middelburg, where the ground is difficult and where Boers were frequently seen.

At a place called Uitkyk, five miles from Middelburg, a place with a bad name in those days, fifty men of the 18th Hussars from Middelburg, were stationed. Not expecting to see any Boers, I went out with my lunch, my walking-stick-gun, and my bird-skinning instruments, expecting to spend a quiet day, and add to my collection of birds.

Leaving groups to picquet important points along the line, we joined up with the 18th Hussars early in the morning at a point seven miles from Olifants River and six from Middelburg. At 9.30 a.m. I was talking to a sergeant of the 18th Hussars. We had seen Kitchener's train leave Olifants River, when we heard shots in the direction of Uitkyk. Looking up we saw at Uitkyk Station about three hundred mounted men in closish formation, galloping as hard as they could. It was impossible to distinguish them at a mile off. It was a most unusual formation for Boers. Subalterns do not like stopping commanders-in-chief for nothing, but I knew there were only fifty of the 18th Hussars, and felt these must be Boers.

All the time the two trains were getting nearer. I had only fourteen men with me; the leading train was quite close, within rifle shot of the Boers. I sent a man galloping back to stop the train, saying I would let them know as soon as I was certain they were Boers, and galloped down myself with a dozen men to a cutting in the line between the Boers and the train. When the Boers saw the train stop, fifty or more came galloping straight for it, and for us hidden in our cutting.

All doubt was now removed, so, telling my men to shoot for all they were worth, I galloped my pony, stumbling and shying at rails and sleepers, six hundred yards down the line to where the first train was. This proved to be an advanced train with a small escort on it, the chief's train was behind, and now closing up to it I told the officer in command that there were fully three hundred Boers close to, and asked him to get both trains back as quickly as possible, saying I would do what I could to delay the Boers.

Galloping back to my men, I was relieved to find that the Boers, not knowing our strength, and having had at least one saddle emptied, had for a time retired back to Uitkyk. We pushed on to try and see what was happening to within long range of Uitkyk, where we could see fully two hundred mounted men buzzing about like bees. Leaving Corporal Stokes and one man hidden here in observation, with orders to fall back on us if the Boers advanced, I sent back to report that the Boers had possession of two miles of the line at Uitkyk, and retired myself to take up a positron in the rear.

Later, thinking my new position seven miles from Olifants River was too isolated, and hearing shots fired on my left, where, owing to the ground, I had scouts out, I retired back to a strong position 1000 yards further back. Before retiring I sent two men to call in Corporal Stokes, but they returned almost immediately under fire without having reached him. They said the Boers had crept along the line, and were now between us and Corporal Stokes. I feared it was all up with Stokes and the other man, as not having enough men, I had no option but to retire.

We retired just in time, for some of the Boers had already sneaked round us by a *donga*, and would very soon have had us in difficulties. When we had got a new and very good position, we lay anxiously waiting and covering Stokes' retirement. Presently we saw three of our men galloping back under fire towards us. Sergeant Ross had, without my knowing it, galloped forward about a mile between two fires and brought both in safely. It was a fine thing to do, and he was recommended for it

The firing on our left had been at one of our men, Private Rose, who was sent by Lord Kitchener with an order for me. Rose had mistaken for me a Boer in khaki on a grey pony, who had made our private signal with his rifle, and had only seen his mistake when within thirty yards of three Boers. They fired and missed him, but he had a narrow escape, and was so full of his own adventures when he reached me, and so out of breath, that it was some time before I could gather what his original message from the chief had been. The message was that a column was coming out from Middelburg, that I was to watch the Boers and report when the line was clear.

We took up a strong position, five miles from Olifants River, and felt our way occasionally from there, but there were too many Boers for us. About noon we saw a man sneaking forward, and thinking he was a Boer, gave him a volley; he dropped apparently dead as a stone. About 12.30 we pushed on again, and coming up to the place where the man had dropped, found him lying very low but alive and well, a scared trooper of the 18th, a recruit just out from home. He had earlier in the day fallen an easy prey to the Boers, who had relieved him of horse, saddle, rifle and *bandolier*, and released him. Luckily we had missed him. His first experience of soldiering had been a lively one.

We pushed on got into touch with the 18th Hussars, and then sent men along the line to see if it had been damaged. About 2 p.m. the Boers seemed to have retired to a farm three miles south of the line. I sent a man to report,

While we were waiting for the trains, we heard from the 18th that 500 Boers had attacked them, and that they had had thirty casualties.

The two trains came on again; the leading one with the escort had passed us, and was puffing and winding up the hill when there was an explosion, and the first train came to a stop. "That's awkward," I thought, "for me, after reporting clear,"—however, it is quite impossible for any but an expert to see a cleverly-hidden mine, and moreover this was not on my section of the line. I sent a sergeant back to the commander-in-chief's train to warn him, but he brought his train (which also had a small escort) right on up to the disabled train.

After putting picquets out round the train we went to have a look at the chief, whom I had not seen properly before. He got out of his saloon, looked at the damage, and seeming much annoyed at the delay, he gave some order and then went back to the carriage. He never seemed to look in the direction of the Boers, who were visible at Trichard's farm only three miles away. I saw Watson and Congreve here, who were on Kitchener's staff. The explosion had luckily missed the engine and the troop's trucks, and gone off under an empty truck.

The column came out from Middelburg, and with its guns sent the Boers away. After a delay of twenty minutes it was found that it would take twenty-four hours to repair the damage, so the chief went straight back to Pretoria.

Next day, January 24th, the same commando, about 400 men (the Heidelburg Commando, Jack Hindon's and Carl Trichard's bands), again attacked the 18th Hussars at Uitkyk, and also drove in one of ray patrols. I saw it from my tent, and while my men were saddling-up, galloped up to the hill where the long-range gun was. The sergeant and most of the gunners were away, so we had to manage with one gunner, one driver, and some men of the Leicester Regiment. The first shot at 7000 yards fell 1000 yards short; however, this and a few more sent the Boers away from the line. We galloped out with about thirty men, but they were too strong for us, and we had to wait till a column again came out from Middelburg, The Boers hung about till the column arrived, but did not blow up the line. We got back to camp late after a long day.

On January 26th we got a telegram from Colonel Campbell congratulating us on our doings on the 23rd, which message gave great pleasure. Another welcome message which came that day was an order to march with all our belongings to Middelburg, where the company was to concentrate for the coming move.

On the 27th we were joined at Middelburg by the Witbank, and on the 29th by the Pan detachments. The big move was at last coming. None of us knew what the move was to be, but we were in it With a fine company of 120 men, and under our own most popular colonel, we were to form part of one of those many columns with which General French was going to turn the tide of the war.

General French's Mounted Infantry crossing the Vaal at Viljoen's Drift

PART 5

February 1st to April 27th, 1901

The move commonly known as "French's Eastern Trek" would, if carried out as originally conceived, have gone very near ending the war. It was to have been a sweep of nine columns from westwards on to the Swaziland border to the east. But at the last moment two strong columns under Generals Plumer and Paget, which were to have been on the left of the sweeping line, were called off to attend to De Wet, who had broken into Cape Colony. Thus only seven columns were available, and there was a large gap on the left of the line, with nothing but the small column under Colonel Campbell to fill it. Through this gap most of the Boers, among them the commandos of Beyers and Louis Botha, eventually escaped.

The movement ended in the capture of over 2000 Boers, and numbers of guns, waggons, cattle and sheep; and in a great clearing of a country which up till then had been untouched; and even as it was, it caused such a change in the tone of the Boer commandos that in April, with the prospect of winter before them, they sent Louis Botha to meet Lord Kitchener at Middelburg, and almost agreed to the terms he then offered them.

There was little fighting during this movement, but the column under Colonel Campbell, owing to its isolated position and to its weakness in numbers, saw most of what fighting there was; and some idea of the whole may be gathered from the following diary, which, with all its faults, I reproduce almost as written on the spot from day to day.

Friday, February 1st, 1901.—Lynes having had an accident at the last moment, his place was taken by Legard. Left at 6 a.m. with Legard, Reade and 114 men, as good a lot as one could want. Column consisted of Leicesters 900 strong, two squadrons 18th Hussars, one section 21st Field Battery R.A. under Major Corbyn, one long-range 12-pounder gun, and one pom-pom. Total about 1200 men under Col. W. Pitcairn-Campbell, King's Royal Rifles. A few Boers sniped at us on the way, but were soon shifted with the help of the pom-pom under Capt. Poole, and we camped at Bankfontein, twelve miles south of Middelburg.

Saturday, February 2nd.—Lost two horses from horse-sickness. Major Laming, 18th Hussars, in command of mounted troops. Left Bankfontein 6 a. m, Legard with one section to do rear guard, remaining three sections escort to pom-pom and support to 18th Hussars advance guard.

Soon after starting, heavy firing to our left, and twelve Boers retired in front of us. Soon after, twenty Boers on our right also retired in front of us, taking up a position on a high hill to our right front.

Advanced slowly, Boers sniping all the time. This high ridge towards Wolverfontein had to be attacked. The pom-pom and M.I. were halted, while Capt, Pollock's squadron 18th Hussars advanced on foot, and well extended, like good infantry under fire, while shells from our three guns covered their advance, bursting beautifully just in front of the Hussars as they pushed on. They cleared the Boers from this ridge, but another long ridge ran out from this one to our left,

A troop of 18th was scouting this other ridge when it got sniped at and Major Laming told me to send a section under an officer to reinforce. Reade was the only officer. His orders were to go to the left of 18th and work on from there. We were 2000 yards in rear with the pom-pom. As I launched this section out, I galloped with Reade on one side and Sergt. Burton on the other, explaining what was wanted.

They went on to where the 18th were, and were met by an officer, and dismounted, as far as I could see, among the 18th. The 18th mounted and advanced on horseback. They had only gone a short way when there was a heavy fire and some confusion. The Hussars came back to where Reade's led horses were in rear of his men. At this time it was impossible for us to see what was going on; we came under an accurate fire ourselves, and we could not for the life of us make out which were Boers. The pom-pom was with us, and luckily was not moved forward or fired.

What happened was this: Causton's troop of 18th, owing to some mistake, advanced without giving scouts time to get out, and rode straight into a position strongly held by about thirty Boers. They came back, losing Causton and five men. Reade—who was just behind a slight rise with his men dismounted, his horses left under cover behind the rise—shouted "Advance!"

Possibly he might have come off better if he had retired a little and held the rise in the ground behind him, but one cannot say so for certain, and no officer of far greater experience could be blamed for acting as he did, being under a sudden and deadly fire at the time. With twelve men he advanced, got down and fired, and fought gallantly. The fire must have been terrible, for out of his twelve men only five got away, and all were hit or grazed in more places than one. When Reade was hit, he shouted to his men to retire, and Sergt. Burton, also mortally wounded, repeated the order.

Corpl. Thomson and four men fell back fighting, to their horses, which had been steadily held by Corpl. Stokes and his men, also under fire. The moment it was seen that they were in difficulties, Sergt. Allen with his section galloped half-left, and, dismounting under fire, worked right round Reade's left, and at fifty yards shot three Boers, and drove off the rest who were looting the dead and wounded. I had sent two men mounted, to watch Reade's left, and they both had their horses hit. One was itching to be doing something, but being tied to the pom-pom which was also under fire, and it being impossible to make out what was going on, it was a trying moment. According to the "rules of war" these thirty Boers should not have been where they were, for they were completely outflanked by Pollock's squadron. But one might as well try to outflank flies as Boers, who have no base to retire to, and no waggons or encumbrances to watch.

When Sergeant Allen had worked round, we got orders to advance. It was a terrible sight that waited me. Passing two dead troopers of the 18th, then Corporal Oldham whom I had known as a good soldier since he joined my Company in 1895, I came upon Bullock—quite a boy—in great pain, dismounted and gave him a drink, and left a man to look after him. Then about fifty yards further on, just over a slight rise, I came upon Reade, Sergeant Burton, Freeman, Parnham, and one of the 18th—all still alive but badly hit. I couldn't stop till I had made good the ground in front of me, so posting some men to hold the place, came back. I found poor Reade badly hit in both arms and one hand, with Hardy, the doctor to the 18th Hussars, attending to him.

Sergeant Burton was lying dead with one arm round Reade; he had evidently been helping him when he was shot through the heart himself. About ten yards to the left was Freeman, a veteran of the Matabele war, with eight wounds and in very great pain. He said, "Oh! Mr. Crum, send me the doctor," and died immediately after. I then went and turned over a body ten yards to Reade's right, and found Parnham (a very good boy, and one who had shot a Boer at Vredefort) with a bullet through his forehead. I knelt over him; he was too bad to drink. I told him quietly that he had done gallantly, and a faint smile of pleasure came over his face. I think these were the last words he heard, though he went on breathing for twenty-four hours.

I then went back to Reade with a very heavy heart. He was quite conscious, and seemed a little afraid he had made a mistake, but we told him how splendidly he had done. He was very thirsty, and I gave him tea from a water-bottle; he was wandering a little, and said the tea was not hot enough. Then he said, "Well, anyway, this is better than being at Pan." I turned aside terribly cut up and crying like a child. The infantry came up, and then the ambulances. When I went back to Reade, Hardy was still attending to him.

It was a curious thing that we three should all be together again and under such similar circumstances. Reade who seemed easier now said, "Last time we met, you were hit, and Hardy and I were looking after you." He told me the Boers had taken his carbine and glasses, and one of them had given him a drink, but had refused to bandage his arm which was bleeding, when he, powerless with both, had asked the Boer to help him. One can't blame the Boer, for he was under fire at the time, and very soon had to go as fast as he could. This small party of Boers seem to have fought bravely, to give them their due, though they did use expanding bullets.

Colonel Campbell pushed right on with his infantry, covering an enormous front, and advanced on Roodepoort Farm. There had been about 300 Boers laagered in this neighbourhood. They were under Ghos and Trichard, and were the same lot who had given us so much trouble at Pan and Uitkyk. About 4.30 p.m., I got into camp, after posting Cossack-posts, and securing four sheep for the men on the way. I was tired and sad, but there was consolation in the fact that the men had done well. As for poor Reade, who had been so keen and jolly twenty-four hours before, I felt it terribly. Sergeant Burton, an Indian veteran and reservist with two medals, was due to return home by the next ship to his wife and children at Winchester. We also had hit this day Allen, Epps, and three horses.

Sunday, February 3rd.—Remained in camp at Roodepoort. Boers thought that we would move, and made an attack on what they took to be our rear guard; other parties in front and on flanks. About 400 Boers appeared suddenly at 8.30 a.m. about 6000 yards from our camp to the west I saw them first and reported to the Colonel, who opened fire on them from camp with our three guns, and brought down several before they got out of range. We saddled-up and went down to water. An order came for us to reinforce the Leicester post about two miles north of camp. The Boers had worked round and were threatening this post, taking it to be our rear guard. A company of the Leicesters, like old soldiers and good ones that they are, had entrenched themselves and held their own well.

We advanced at a gallop for about a mile-and-a-half, and, dismounting, advanced on left of the Leicester post, two sections in firing line, one on left flank, and one in support. The guns from camp covered our advance well, pitching shrapnel just in front of us as we pushed on. In spite of this there were a good many bullets about, and we had to creep up, covering each others' advance. The Leicesters had one or two men hit, but we had none. About 11 a.m. the Boers retired, having completely failed in their attempt, and having lost many men. They left look-out posts all round us all the rest of the day.

This small column is surrounded, and the sooner it gets in touch with Alderson's and Smith-Dorrien's columns the better, though it is a real good column and in good hands. Poor Reade had his finger off, but was too weak to have his arm off. The sad thing is that, under the circumstances, all the wounded have to be brought along with us, and the jolting of the waggons must kill some of them. We cannot spare an ambulance, as more are sure to be needed tomorrow. The Boers have cut our field telegraph wire, but we can heliograph to Pan, and have sent all details to Reade's people that way.

No signs of other columns. We start tomorrow at 5 a.m., and expect an anxious fifteen miles' march. We buried Lieutenant Causton and four men of the 18th Hussars, and Sergeant Burton and three men of the King's Royal Rifles just outside the farm at Roodepoort Colonel Campbell himself read the service, and we left temporary wooden crosses over the graves. At 6 p.m. the colonel explained his orders and intentions to us all. He had an anxious job before him, but showed little sign of worry, and filled us with confidence. I sent in this day the name of Private Pedrick for gallantry on February 2nd. On that occasion he advanced with his section under fire, and borrowing a water-bottle and field-dressing from two of the men, crept right on 200 yards beyond his own section to where Private Hughes of the 18th Hussars was lying wounded. He gave the trooper a drink, attended to his wound, and kept the Boers off.

Monday, February 4th.—We had felt anxious about our next advance, fifteen miles from Roodepoort to Bosman's Pan. The 400 Boers who attacked us on Sunday were last seen on our front, other commandos were reported, and we expected to be harassed all the way, However at daybreak, when we advanced, there was hardly a Boer to be seen. I went with two sections on the left flank, and sent Legard with the other two with the pom-pom. We got to Bosmansfontein without fighting, clearing the country and bringing many Boer ladies and families along with us on their waggons.

A party of Canadians from General Alderson s column joined us here They gave us the impression that Alderson's column was quite near, and I, for once was much relieved. In reality these sportsmen were quite on their own, and nowhere near their own column, and we were on the point of fighting a small battle with Chris Botha.

The transport halted at Bosmansfontein till about 1 p.m. It had just moved on, and got over the rise into the valley of Klein Olifants River, when a high-velocity gun from a high ridge, six miles off above Bosman's Pan, opened fire on us. This was quite unexpected. It turned out to be Chris Botha with 600 men. We had struck a new commando, luckily the other had gone off south-east and bothered us no more.

The colonel went straight at them. The Leicesters in extended lines covered an enormous front, and looked like swarms of ants. A Boer pom-pom opened—another surprise—but the ants went steadily on, at the top of a tremendous fusillade. I thought the losses would be heavy, but we only had four men wounded here. We were halted on the left flank of the baggage, fully five miles from this battle, so that it was difficult to realise what was going on. Several shells from the high-velocity gun landed among us and the waggons, but never bursting properly did no damage.

I saw a shell burst near one of my men who was sitting on an ant-heap holding his horse; he merely turned his head round and laughed to his nearest neighbour. I did not feel so confident myself, but then

I had not been through the siege of Ladysmith. At last the waggons moved on to Bosman's Pan, and we on the left advanced to Morrison's store, which we held against a great many snipers.

When I got into camp, worried and tired after a long day, I went with Colonel Campbell to see how Reade had stood the journey, and to my great grief found that he had died just ten minutes before. I had got so fond of the boy in the short time I had known him, and to see him lying there was a solemn moment, which I shall never forget. The Boers were shelling and pom-pomming the camp and sniping all round it, so it was a question where and how to bury him. I went out about 400 yards from camp, and chose a nice place above Bosman's Pan where there was luckily no sniping. The men of his own section coming in off picquet rode as escort to the grave, where Colonel Campbell himself read the service, and we all came back very sad over so great a loss. One or two shots fell among our horses as we returned.

Tuesday, February 5th.—Advanced to De Wette Krans, about fourteen miles south on the Ermelo Road, my company on rear guard, which is difficult work with so few officers. Small parties of Boers rode along just out of range. Legard's first position was at Reade's grave, and his men put stones round it and a temporary cross. It was strange to be fighting over the grave of a brother officer, who two days before had been so keen and happy. We got touch with General Alderson's column about 9 a.m., and did not meet with any serious opposition. The country was full of good farms, and the men have all had good dinners tonight, chickens, ducks, turkeys, and geese. All women and children are being brought along with the column. They tell of twelve Boers wounded in yesterday's fight, and many more on Sunday. We are encamped at Groebelar's Farm, a very decent spot.

There is a large interval between us and Smith-Dorrien to our left which I should like to see filled. A Canadian scout starts tonight to go to Smith-Dorrien[1] he says he does not know the road, but intends to catch a *burgher* and make him show the way.

Wednesday, February 6th.—Left De Wette Krans, being called at 3.30, breakfasts at 4 a.m., left 4.30. On the high ground a mile from camp got into thick mist, and the column halted for an hour till it cleared. We heard Smith-Dorrien's guns at Lake Chrissie. My company got split up and all over the place, and the men seemed to be rather stupid

---

1. *Smith-Dorrien* by Horace Smith-Dorrien, also published by Leonaur

somehow, possibly owing to the early start and big dinners overnight; anyway, they and the whole column seemed "a bit off." It was difficult working over a hundred mounted men without officers.

We moved over some mountainous country and had a bit of sniping. Fifty Boers came up to within 1500 yards of me, all in a heap and without seeing us. I did not fire as I preferred to warn the column first, and as I could not see how many more there might be. We got the guns on to them but they were slow and didn't do any good.

One sniper near Hartebeest Spruit braved the whole column, and rather upset theories as to the deadliness of modern arms. I was sitting talking to Wills of the 18th Hussars, who had a troop dismounted in advance of my company, when from a ridge about 1000 yards off— "*ping-pong!*"—and my grey pony shied off as a bullet hit the ground at his feet. Back we all got ignominiously to where my company was, and from the cover returned the fire at 1800 yards, but with no effect on our sportsman, who kept up his firing with quiet regularity. The pom-pom opened, then the Leicesters of the advance guard, and next two guns and two maxims— all firing at this one Boer, who only occasionally showed his head.

When there was a lull in our firing we heard the *pick-pock* of his Mauser, and a bullet close to someone was a signal like a wasp's sting for a renewed fusillade on our part The climax was reached when the sportsman, standing boldly up, folded his arms and defied us while you could have counted twenty. After a delay of about fifteen minutes a party of the 18th went round one way and we went round the other to try and cut our friend off, but only arrived in time to see him and five others ride off alive and well!

We pushed on as far as Klipstapel on the Ermelo-Carolina Road, a high point with a grand view, where I left a picquet and returned to camp. From Klipstapel we saw considerable numbers of Boers in the distance trekking in a north-westerly direction. These were the commandos of Beyers, Botha, and others, who after attacking Smith-Dorrien at Lake Chrissie had broken back between his column and ours.

Thursday, February 7th,—Moved on at 5 a.m. through Klipstapel and Botha's Rust and got into an easier country. At Mooiplatz Farm we got into touch with General Alderson's mounted troops[2] on our right, and Colonel Henry's [3] on our left. In the farm we found a dozen

---

2. 12th and 13th M.I.
3. 5th Lancers, 3rd M.I., and 2nd I.L.H. (Smith-Dorrien's column).

badly-wounded Boers, who had been hit in Botha's night-attack on Smith-Dorrien at Lake Chrissie. This seems to have been a very bold thing on the part of Louis Botha, who attacked our 4000 men with his 2000, and under cover of the attack got all his waggons through, passing quite close to the camp. Thus it seems to me he has broken through the net which was being drawn to the Swazi Border, and now threatens our rear and the railway with its short-handed garrisons.

We camped at Bothwell on Lake Chrissie, feeling perfectly safe now with a column on each side of us. I think all of us feel that it was an anxious time coming from Middelburg. The colonel did splendidly; the 18th Hussars, the Leicesters, and the accurate guns of the 21st Battery are thoroughly good, and I think the Canadian scout who came over from Alderson's column was not far wrong when he said our column was "the tidiest little outfit" he had seen, and that "when the colonel gave the word it moved like clockwork and nothing would stop it."

Friday, February 8th.—Halted at the north end of Lake Chrissie, a mile away from General Smith-Dorrien's camp, and about six miles from General Alderson's. Found twenty men for Cossack-posts about two miles and a half from camp; a Boer lookout post just within long range of our posts, but we were content to look at each other. It was very wet and stormy all day, and was very trying for the men. While posting my men I took young Shepherd with me; he was the only one with Reade who got off untouched, and he shot a Boer at ten yards. I told him he had done well, and he said he didn't mind what happened to him now he had got one Boer and done his share. The poor boy's hands were covered with *veldt* sores, and he could hardly hold his reins. He had no coat, as his was torn, so I left him my oilskin coat Went over to tea with Davidson, who is on Smith-Dorrien's staff.

Saturday, February 9th.—Left Bothwell at 4.30. After the very heavy rain the roads were frightful; the waggons got bogged over and over again, and had to be unloaded. The Company did rear guard, which I think the nastiest job of all, particularly when roads are bad and Boers active. Today only a dozen Boers, and they very gentlemanly. Smith-Dorrien's column branched off to our left, and camped seven miles from our new camp at Blauwater. Posted twenty-five men night-picquet; a long and tiring day. We have a 5-inch gun with us now.

Sunday, February 10th.—An easy day from a fighting point of view, but a terrible day for the transport. Their difficulties must be seen to be realised. A long train of waggons, ox and mule, each in its turn getting bogged up to the axles, having to be unloaded and then pulled out with the help of double spans of oxen and mules, and aided by the indefatigable Leicesters, sometimes only to sink again fifty yards further on. Harness and tackle kept breaking, mules became obstinate, and oxen fell out exhausted. So bad was the state of the roads that it was 6,50 p.m, before the last waggon got into Hamilton, only a six or seven mile march.

The farms being well-to-do in these parts, we got large quantities of ducks, geese, pigs, and forage. We saw no Boers, but there were evident traces of a hurried trek, dead oxen, sheep, and abandoned waggons being found in large numbers. We burned at least thirty waggons to-day and lots of forage. Smith-Dorrien's column heliographed that they had captured thirty Boers with waggons and 4000 cattle. Went over to Hamilton Farm with Sergeant Robbins, who was in despair about his waggons, all the swingle-trees and chains having been broken. By good luck we found everything we required in that line, also spades and a Cape cart. The river was in flood, and we had difficulty in crossing.

Monday, February 11th.—A short march to Bonnie Braes. A most glorious view from all the high ground in these parts; saw a large herd of over 1000 buck. Was sent out with thirty men to reconnoitre to Umplasi River, No Boers, but more traces of their hurried trek; we got thousands of sheep. Waggons got on better today.

Tuesday, February 12th.—On rear guard. Waggons, once on high ground, came on well. No Boers for miles around. Camped at Churchill, seven miles. No farms or poultry in these parts; looks a good country for sport. Had to leave thousands of sheep behind. Smith-Dorrien reports 100 waggons, 1000 cattle, and 2300 sheep.

Wednesday, February 13th.—Short and easy march, crossing the drift over Usutu River at Newstead; camped on south side. We found Cossack posts and two escorts, which returned with lots of poultry, etc. I rode to "West ho," Pocock's Farm, about six miles from Amsterdam. From the hills here there is one of the most glorious views in the world, with the Swaziland and Wakerstroom mountains and miles of beautiful country. Could see no Boers. Pocock's Farm was full of mules, horses, and cattle, which the Boers had for some unknown reason left untouched. A man with a Scotch name and his two sons surrendered to us here; they had fought against us, and remembered seeing me at Dundee.

Thursday, February 14th.—Moved about eight miles in, to Amsterdam; a difficult road through a wonderful country, especially the Glen Aggy Pass, which I hope I may someday see again. No Boers. A few Pathans could have given us great trouble in such a country, but the Boer prefers to live for his country rather than die for it.

Amsterdam is a nice little town, lying under the steep slopes to the north. Streams of clear water run down the sides of the streets. There are hedges of fruit trees and jolly gardens, This was the first entry of British troops, and I do not think the inhabitants had much to complain of. But I fear before the war is over it will not be what it is now. The houses were crowded with Boer families left behind in the stampede. The peaches were at their best, and there were lots of poultry and forage for the first comers, Smith-Dorrien's large force with its 300 waggons came in at 5 p.m. The telegraph-line to Piet Retief was in working order, but instead of getting news, as we expected, from General French, we got an unparliamentary reply from a Boer telegraphist.

Friday, February 15th.—Halted at Amsterdam. I visited Stoffel Tosen's Farm. Now Stoffel Tosen was one of those who brought on the war, and his name had been conspicuous in the papers when we were at Maritzburg in 1899, so I had no compunction in taking two of his mules and inspanning them into his Cape cart, which we filled with oat-hay, mealies, apricots, poultry, and other useful things, and drove back to camp.

A deputation of Swazi savages in wonderful get-up, with *assegais* and shields came to see General Smith-Dorrien. They said a great many Boers had come into their country, and their queen wanted to know what to do with them. I saw the deputation go off singing, chanting, and dancing, with a large present of sheep and oxen. It was a good way of disposing of some of the 4000 odd cattle we had collected.

Davidson, the energetic signalling officer to Smith-Dorrien's column, came over to tea and gave us the news. He had been talking to several columns, General French, Colonel Knox, and others, in the direction of Piet Retief. Our picquets came in wet through, but singing and in great spirits, with heavy loads of poultry. Our horses are looking as fit as I ever saw them, the six-pound ration of oats having been supplemented so far by looted forage. No one seems to know what our next move will be.

Saturday, February 16th.—A drizzly wet day; at 12.30 got sudden order to trek with all fit men and horses at 2 p.m., taking three days' rations, and moving as light as possible. A longish march; got into camp at Wolverkop, about ten miles south-east of Amsterdam, where a small detachment of Alderson s column already was. Cold, wet, and uncomfortable arrival in dark, and camping on muddy ground, but we soon settled down like old soldiers, and Faulkner produced a good dinner for Legard and me about 8.30 p.m.

Sunday, February 17th.—Could not move next morning owing to rain and mist Some Boers with guns said to be hiding in *kloofs* about four miles off in a very difficult country. At about 9 a.m. General Alderson came over to consult with Major Laming, They rode out to look at the country, and I went with them to some high ground two miles off, We sat some time looking at the *kloofs* and mountains where the Boers were, and they discussed the best way of doing things, A few Boers sniped from a distance, and were answered by some of Alderson's Mounted Infantry escort. Much interested in meeting General Alderson, who is the chief of my branch—the Mounted Infantry. Very wet all the afternoon, making it beastly for the men with no shelter. Legard and I secured a Boer tent, which kept us fairly dry,

Monday, February 18th.—Another wet misty day made any combined movement impossible. Two Boers, looking very wretched, came in from the *kloofs* and surrendered with rifles and ponies. One was sent back with a letter inviting the rest to surrender, and telling them they would be allowed to keep their stock and stay with their families. They were quite astonished at the terms, having expected to be branded with a broad-arrow and deported to fight in China, and in the course of the day over twenty came in. They say more will come.

I went out with Corporal Casey to meet one lot, who rode up to us with hands extended, saying, "Shake hands, now we will be friends." I shook hands, saying I hoped war would soon be over and that we should all soon be friends. It cheers one up, all these surrenders, and they all seem so sick of the war. Every Burgher and every rifle helps at this stage. I only wish we could get hold of the leaders and it would soon be over. We are running short of rations, biscuits, groceries, and forage, but we have unlimited meat

Tuesday, February 19th.—Wet and misty again, but it cleared up by

8 a.m. and to everyone's satisfaction we got orders to start at 10.15, and, in conjunction with the mounted troops of the other two columns, to round up the Boers in the Swaziland *kloofs*. Four small columns were to close in from opposite directions. We had to occupy a high *kopje* four-and-a-half miles from camp, the one from which there had been some sniping. Our company went at the *kopje* in good style, cantering straight at it in extended order, a few shots from two R.H.A. guns covering our advance.

No shots, no Boers, four casualties from ant-bear holes, but no damage done. From the top there was a grand view of a most mountainous and difficult country, full of ravines, *kloofs*, and dense jungle, reminding one of the hills in India. It was just as well the Boers had surrendered; we could never have found them all in such a country. We found about a dozen waggons and carts hidden in the *kloofs*, and the other columns caught a few Boers and a lot of cattle. I should like to spend a few days in peacetime in this wonderful country; it must be full of game.

Wednesday and Thursday, February 20th and 21st.—Miserable wet days, making a move impossible owing to the mist It is bad enough for Legard and me in our half-waterproof tent, but most uncomfortable for the men in the slush and mud of the lines; however, they are wonderfully cheery. Colonel Campbell and remainder of column joined us, so we are all together again. More Boers surrendered.

Friday, February 22nd.—A thunderstorm and heavy rain at night. Really this rain is getting beyond a joke. All the drifts are impassable, and the roads quite impossible for waggons, so here we are stuck. All the columns are stuck in the same way, and Colonel Burn-Murdoch's convoy of supplies for us all is also stuck. We are sending out to collect all available *mealies*.

About 2 p.m. (raining hard) I was sent with twenty men to bring in some Boers and cattle, marked down by a *Kaffir*, quite close he said. It turned out a long way and a desperate climb, and we did not get back till 9 p.m. I had two guides and some *Kaffirs*. We made a long *détour* to keep out of sight, and left our horses at the top of a hill four miles from camp. Then our troubles began. I had stupidly got gum-boots on; we went on for about three miles, and down about 1500 feet over rocks and through jungle. Reaching a precipice we looked over and saw one of the Boers with a rifle guarding a herd of cattle.

Leaving men at each of the two possible exits from this ravine, the guides, four men, and I stalked down, most of the time in full view of the Boer with the cattle. It was a long and difficult descent, about 500 feet, and the Boer ought to have seen or heard us, for what with rocks falling, twigs cracking, and ammunition boots, our attempts at stalking were not good. We only moved when his back was turned, and each of us crouched and kept still at a signal.

Thus we passed within 200 yards of him and he never saw us. Beyond him was the smoke of a *laager*; we did not know how many Boers there might be and wanted to surprise them before they could use their rifles. About ten yards off we rushed the *laager*—and found only one Boer in it, an old chap with his Mauser by his side and *bandoliers* on him. The guide made a good deal of noise shouting, "Hands up!" and rushed on to the other Boer with the cattle, who also put his hands up. It would have been better to do the thing quietly, for there might have been others about. However, these were all there were, so we started back with them, two good ponies, rifles and ammunition, and 120 head of fine cattle. It was a grand stalk, as good as any sportsman could wish for.

It was nearly dark when we started to return, and we had a terrible climb over very rough ground before we got back to our ponies. Every minute ft got darker. The men very soon got beat, and my gum-boots handicapped me badly. We shared the Boer ponies and carried the extra rifles in turn, the Boers driving their own cattle, and after many long rests, feeling more dead than alive, we got back to our ponies about 8 p.m. pitch-dark. I never felt much more beat, having to lift my legs up with my hands; my right arm, which gets rheumatic in wet weather, was on this occasion quite useless to me. We got into camp after 9, and found the colonel, who had been a little anxious about us, very pleased to hear of our success. Faulkner had got a good dinner waiting for me and dry clothes. Very tired; slept splendidly.

Saturday, February 23rd.—Very stiff after yesterday; out all morning with the 18th and pom-pom, but saw no Boers.

Sunday, February 24th.—The 18th Hussars surprised a Boer down the *kloof*, and found six carts and buggies and the Amsterdam Commando flag. Legard got a good four-wheeled spider. Rain seems to be clearing at last. Got a milk-cow and she is doing us well. We are running short of supplies, no forage or groceries after today, but so long as we have *mealies* and sheep and tobacco we are right enough.

Monday, February 25th.—At last we leave our muddy camp at Wolvenkop. Searched *kloofs* again in the morning, and then moved camp to Shela River, ten miles north of Piet Reteif. Can't cross the *drift* yet, must wait till the river subsides. Dined with the colonel.

Tuesday, February 26th.—Shela River still in flood, but going down; some of us swam horses across. The sun shone all day, and gave us all a most welcome chance of getting dry and clean after so much rain and mud. The Leicesters and R. Engineers made a foot-bridge and a wire trolly-ferry. Visits from Shaw, Stirling, and Majendie from General Alderson's camp, which is at Derby, only three miles off. In the afternoon I rode over to tea with Majendie, General Alderson's camp spreads over a lot of ground, detachments being some miles out from the main camp. General Smith-Dorrien, on the other hand, had his huge camp all packed close together at Lake Chrissie, and the night-picquets very close to the camp. I prefer our camp, which is a compromise between the two, the picquets digging trenches each night at intervals of one to four hundred yards, and forming a circle round the camp at a distance of about three-quarters of a mile according to the ground

Wednesday, February 27th.—An early start; after three hours all waggons were got across the *drift*. My company rear guard did not leave camp till Smith-Dorrien's advance guard arrived, so that I met Colonel Henry, commanding the mounted troops of that column, Colonel King, and some of the 5th Lancers, whom I had not seen since Maritzburg days. About three miles on we passed through Alderson's camp at Derby, and, four miles further, through Colonel Knox's camp (10th Hussars, 12th Lancers, and 14th Hussars).

After a march of about twelve miles we got into Piet Retief, which was full of General French's troops, waiting for the arrival of the convoy from Volksrust They had all been very short of rations for a long time. I think we had fared better than most, owing to Colonel Campbell saving his supplies while we were passing through the land of plenty. The sunshine after so much rain, the interest of seeing so many columns and old friends, and of seeing a new place, made it an eventful day; but what made it a worthy commemoration of Paardeberg was the arrival of a wire to General French from Lord Kitchener, saying that he was at Middelburg, awaiting Louis Botha to arrange terms of peace, and that De Wet had been driven out of Cape Colony, losing all his guns.

Thursday, February 28th.—Halted at Piet Retief. Saw Majors Bird and Lowndes of Dublin Fusiliers, who had been wounded at Talana; also Miles Tristram, who dined (if one can use the word) and went to a concert got up by Major Corbyn, 21st R.A. Concert a great success, with a piano on a platform made of waggons. Closed it by singing, for the first time, "God save the King!"

Friday, March 1st.—Moved on twelve miles south-east of Piet Retief to block the Sandbank Drift over the Assegai River. Colonel Allenby's column with Scots Greys on opposite side of the river. Eddie Ussher came over to tea with us, and shared our last ration of tea and last pot of jam. He said his column had been out of such luxuries for days. We seem likely to remain here some time,

Saturday, March 2nd.—Climbed hill 700 feet above camp, where we had a company of Leicesters encamped; a grand view for miles, and heliograph communication to Wakkerstroom. Colonel Henry heliographed that he had caught sixty Boers and twenty-four waggons. Heavy thunder-showers came through our tent and made things uncomfortable. Out of tobacco. This is a poor place to stop at with scarcity of wood and *mealies*.

Sunday, March 3rd.—Took a patrol about six miles into Swaziland border with guides, A very nice ride over mountain tracks; no Boers about; only one farm, and that a very poor one, with a lot of Boer women and children who were living on green *mealies* and sugar cane. Rode back over some very rough ground, lovely streams of pure water, ferns and flowers but no trees; a lot of Swazis with assegais, no clothes, living in scattered *kraals* with patches of green *mealies*. Dined with the Colonel.

Monday, March 4th.—Sending some of the worst horses back to the line; we have too many, as so many men have gone sick, most of them from veldt sores. (130 horses to 95 men.)

Tuesday, March 5th.—Moved camp to Krogh's Concession, well in Swaziland. Starting 5 a.m. waggons got in 2 p.m. Rain made roads very bad, and we had to make a drift On rear guard, wet and very cold. This weather is beastly, and gives me rheumatism in my arm. The ration biscuits are very hard; as only my front teeth are any use to me, and as I have toothache in the only molars left, I am in a bad way. It would be interesting seeing this country if one could see it, but with the mist one sees nothing.

Wednesday, March 6th.—Reached Umshengi Drift, on Assegai River, about 2.30 p.m. One of the worst roads and wettest days we have had. It is a marvel how these waggons get along at all, up to the axles in mud most of the way.

Thursday, March 7th.—Heavy rain all night, and no sign of it clearing; ready to start at 7; orders came, "No trek"; very glad; this weather is ghastly.

Friday, March 8th.—Rain not quite so bad. Returned Krogh's Concession, took a patrol about six miles east to top of a very high hill where I had seen two mounted men and some loose horses. Caught two wild ponties; extensive view, and all country seemed clear; no roads, only *Kaffir* tracks over very mountainous country.

Saturday, March 9th.—A welcome interval of sun. Trekked back to Sandbank Drift. Ten Boers and five waggons surrendered, reporting that they had been treacherously attacked by Swazis, who had killed fourteen. This was important news. Though one does not like the Swazis joining in, it is not our fault if the Boers go into Swaziland. The Boers challenged us to fight. Let them fight us or surrender, and not run away into Swaziland. We are on the telegraph-wire again. It does not seem that Botha has made peace. However, with fine weather our spirits are up.

Sunday and Monday, March 10th and 11th.—Two more wet days. Went out with twelve men and guides to try and catch two Boers hiding near Umshenga's. Two Basutos did the scouting for us, and astonished me by the wonderful way they got about on their ponies. One minute we saw them at the top of what looked like an inaccessible mountain, and shortly after caught sight of them again so far away from their last position that it seemed to be someone else. They always went just where one wanted. The Boer and the Natal guide, too, seemed to get over the country much better than we could. They never got off or rested their horses; they were heavier men and had smaller ponies, and yet they could leave us standing.

We came on a Cape boy who had lived at his hut since 1883. He told us of some Boers and guns in Swaziland. He said he didn't trust the Swazis, who were more afraid of the Boers than of us, and would not help us; that the Swazis were getting very cheeky, being all armed with assegais, which is forbidden by the Boers; but that they were a cowardly lot, and would confine themselves to stealing cattle.

Returned by Potgieter's Farm, which had evidently been a good house once, with a piano, a four-poster bed, etc. There was a good garden, with figs, oranges, and green mealies, two cats and some ducks. Leaving three men to lookout, I stayed an hour here, turning the horses into the mealies and the men into the fruit. Got home about 4.30, after pleasant enough day in spite of the rain. My oilskin and sou'wester have done good service this trek; I will mention them in despatches. It seems likely we shall stay at Sandbank, blocking the drift, for some time on short rations.

Monday and Tuesday, March 12th and 13th.—Seems to be clearing, A few English papers of February 2nd arrived. We hear Botha has gone to meet Steyn and others to arrange terms. All in great spirits; dined with the colonel, who gave us an excellent dinner for such hard times,

Wednesday, March 14th,—A glorious fine day. The Swazis have been going for the Boers again, causing many to surrender to us. Eddie Ussher came over again, crossing the Assegai on the trolly-ferry which we had put up. He had just heard of his promotion.

Corbyn pleased us by saying that he had soldiered with a great many cavalry and mounted infantry regiments on both sides of the country—the O.R.C. and Natal—but that he had never seen a lot of men who took better care of their horses than our men did. The horses lately have been in a very bad way, but we now get two pounds of oats a day, and with fine weather and plenty of green *mealies* they will improve. The want of shoes is serious; except for that we could mount all our men on fit horses.

Thursday, March 15th.—At 7 a.m. the Swazi Chief Umshenga sent in to say that forty Boers had crossed the Assegai River at his *drift*, where they were off-saddled, with their horses quite done up. The messengers got to us at 9 a.m. One squadron 18th Hussars, sixty-five of us, the pom-pom, and a company of Leicesters were ordered to start at once, with transport for one night. Unfortunately we waited for the Leicesters and the transport, and did not get off till 10.30 a.m. About 1 p.m. we were within two miles of the *kloof* where the Boers were, when *Kaffirs* came and told us they were saddling-up. The 18th Hussars then pushed on, and coming on the tail of the Boers, with the help of the guides and Swazis, chased them for some distance over very rough ground, killing two and catching eight, among them some Staat's Artillery and Swazi police. They also got some ponies and mules.

In the meantime we branched off to the left to try and head them off at the only *drift* available for them to escape by. After some mistakes we got on to a track leading to the drift, and took up a position—sixty of us and the pom-pom—commanding a point which our guide said the Boers must pass to get away. Presently we saw thirty Boers and ponies about 5000 yards off, evidently going to the drift. After waiting for a bit, it was evident that our guide was wrong; and that the Boers would not pass our way; then we lost sight of them.

The road down to the drift was through a nasty country, steep mountains on each side, and once in this defile one had to take considerable risks. We pushed on about a mile-and-a-half down. Again our guide said we must get an easy shot from where we were at any Boers crossing the *drift*, and that they must come our way; so again we waited. Still no Boers. Then one of my men, who had climbed up 600 feet above us, shouted down to us, "They are crossing the *drift*," but it was getting late, so we did not follow them up. I went on with four men another mile-and-a-half to a *kopje*, which we climbed, and found to be only 1000 yards from the *drift*.

If only we had known the country, this was the place we should have made for. It was a great disappointment—thirty Boers, each with two ponies, and only missed by a few minutes. They had come down a regular precipice to keep out of sight of us, and had just got away. If we had been quicker in the morning, or if we had only been a bit bolder in going right down to the *drift*! This was certainly a case for pushing; but pushing and thrusting when Boers are about has often proved fatal, and men who thrust at the right time are few and far between. We had a long way to get back in the dark; our horses, after living so much on green mealies, were done up, and we only got back to Potgieter's Farm, where we camped, at 10 p.m. We lost three of our horses.

Saturday, March 17th.—Changed places with the other squadron of the 18th Hussars, and returned to Sandbank Drift. One company of Leicesters and the 18th Hussars remained at Potgieter's to watch the Umshenga Drift General French wired to say, "Very pleased with the 18th and K.R.R. M.I., who must have done well." A convoy under Colonel Bullock (now known as "No-surrender Bullock") is expected shortly. Horses must have oats and shoes if they are to do this hard work.

Sunday, March 18th.—Got up early to post picquets; a lovely fine morning—too good to last, as it proved later. Legard and I went down to the drift to see the Boers who had surrendered cross it. There were fifty waggons and more families and a lot of cattle.

The *drift* was about four feet deep in places, and a very strong current. It was a wonderful sight to see how the Boers managed what would have seemed to us impossible. Sixteen oxen all carried off their legs, A Boer, naked and bare-footed, swimming or standing on the stony bottom, tugging at the leading span of oxen, while others, standing well up to their middles in the river, yelled, shouted and flogged the oxen. Sometimes a lot of oxen seemed hopelessly mixed up, but the Boers saw at once what was wrong, and put them right in a very short time.

At times the waggons looked as if they must go over, but someone always did the right thing at the critical moment and saved mishap. The Boer women and children sat with all their belongings in the waggons, and showed no signs of anxiety. Occasionally a chair, table, chicken or other article was washed down the stream in the flood, but the *Kaffirs* were on them at once, and swimming like powerful fish, brought them back to the owners, who received them stolidly, without a 'thank-you' or a look of satisfaction.

As soon as each waggon was across It was outspanned, and the "*vrou*" lit a fire and had something waiting for her man. Once or twice one of the lighter carts did upset, and was overturned and carried, horses and all, down the stream; but the occupants jumped out and swam, and with the help of others the conveyance was dragged ashore, upside-down or sideways, no matter. On the opposite bank the cart was righted, the owner jumped in and drove on, thinking it a grand joke. Now we see how De Wet can give us the slip at a *drift*.

The river kept rising. After two hours a waggon got badly stuck; some loose cattle and horses, driven across higher up the stream, were carried into the waggon and its team. There was the greatest confusion, which was put right with difficulty, and at last operations had to be suspended. A storm was coming. Legard and I had just got back to camp when it burst. Our tent collapsed on the top of us with the first gust, and we were deluged with rain and hail. The worst storm I have ever seen while it lasted. Thunder, lightning and sharp-edged hailstones bigger than racquet balls. One gave me a stunning whack on the head as I was crouching under the *débris* of the tent. I put my hands up to save my head, when I got a most painful rap over the knuckles.

It was "real beastly," and yet while we just crouched under the thin canvas, wet through, we roared with laughter at each other. When it got a bit better we crawled out, and with the help of servants got the tent up again. Everything, blankets, clothes, boots, all soaked, and no chance of drying them. The horses were grazing, knee-haltered, and so luckily could not stampede far, except one or two loose ones, which were caught again four or five miles off. We spent a wet and uncomfortable night.

Monday and Tuesday, March 19th and 20th.—These two days wet and cold, and no chance of drying our things.

Wednesday, March 21st—Today it cleared up. Went into Piet Retief with twenty-five men as escort to fifty surrendered Boer waggons and twelve prisoners—350 persons, counting women and children. Arrived at 1 p.m.; handed over the Boers, and lunched with some of the general's staff. The general came in later, not overpleased at having 350 Boers to feed when he was short of rations.

A convoy arrived from Volksrust bringing oats, which will be the saving of our horses, also Sergt.-Major Rowat, who is as useful as an officer to me. I was very glad to get him back, and he brought with him a Mauser pistol, a camera, and a large tin of biscuits, all very acceptable.

Very disappointing news of the Peace Conference, saying Botha declines terms. However, now we know where we are, and I trust we shall go for the Boers properly. It is time now, I think, to clear every farm, and remove every family and all stock, and to give no terms. Dined with General Smith-Dorrien, who was very good to me.

Friday, March 23rd.—A long day's reconnoitring. Crossed the Assegai River twice, sending Macnamara, our best swimmer, to see how deep it was.

Saturday and Sunday, March 24th and 25th.—Couldn't sleep, owing to flies, which are very bad in this camp, a plague of blue-bottles and other pests. Went about eight miles, and got two waggon-loads of green *mealies* for the horses. Sent twenty-four men and two sergeants as escorts to convoys. Found eighteen men for two patrols besides eighteen on Cossack-posts and the night- picquets, so the Government is getting its money's worth out of us.

Monday, March 26th,—Received a sackful of letters and parcels, first for a long time, and very welcome; among other things a splendid telescope, breeches, leggings, socks, and three bottles of port wine.

Wednesday, March 28th.—Started at 5.30 a.m. with one man to take an important despatch from General French to Colonel Allenby. My orders were to catch up Major Anley, who, with the 3rd M.I., was on his way to join Colonel Allenby in the Pongola country. It turned out a long ride, and if I had known it was to be so far I should have taken two horses, as the risk of coming on a party of Boers, with one's horse done up, was very great. As it was however the horses, though pretty well done up when we got in, were none the worse after a rest, which did them great credit considering the short rations.

Starting at 5.30 a.m. after a good breakfast, and crossing the Assegai River, we reached the camp of the Lancashire Fusiliers at Mahamba at 7.30 a.m., pushed on another seven miles (making seventeen altogether) and halted; watered, fed, and off-saddled for twenty minutes, hiding ourselves in a donga. The road, which turns east into Swaziland for four miles from Mahamba, then runs due south to the Pongola River. It was a splendid road, good enough for a bicycle, and ran through a fairly open country, with a few farms. These had been completely wrecked by the Swazis. About twelve miles further on we caught up Major Anley's convoy, just as he was inspanning to move another five miles. I gave him the letters, and got a receipt for them. Got a cup of coffee from my old Natal friends, the Dublin Fusiliers, and after a halt of half-an-hour we started slowly back, hoping to reach Mahamba camp that night.

It was 1.30 when we started on the return journey, walking and leading most of the way. At 3.30 we reached a farm eight miles off, where I hid the horses in the trees, grazing and off-saddling. Under weigh again at 4.30, horses going much better for the rest, and in the cool of the evening we were able to trot a bit. Reached Mahamba at 8.30 p.m.; very glad to get in, as also, no doubt, were the horses. Saw no Boers all day, though the *Kaffirs* said there were some about. The distance travelled was fifty miles in fifteen hours. I was not over-tired, but the horses on such short rations could not have done much more. Was very glad of the hospitality of the Lancashire Fusiliers, who looked after us well.

Friday, March 29th.—Left at 6 a.m.; got back to Sandbank at 8.30 a.m., both ponies going well.

Saturday, March 30th.—The rainy season seems about over. Sent Legard and thirty men to Piet Retief; they are part of a reinforcement being sent to meet the convoy from Volksrust.

Sunday, March 31st.—At about 12.30 a.m. I was wakened out of a very good sleep by Colonel Campbell himself, who told me six waggons and fifty Boers were crossing the drift five miles up the Assegai River. I was to go out as strong as I could, and if possible head them off. We could only raise forty men, Legard being away and our night-picquets engaged. In half-an-hour we were all ready. Luckily there was a moon to help us to saddle-up by. The Boers were bound to bring their waggons along a road which joined the Sandbank-Piet Retief road at a point five miles from Piet Retief, seven miles from Sandbank.

The colonel gave me a free hand to do what I thought best He sent fifty infantry in support of us, and telephoned to the 18th Hussars at Potgeiters to send some men from that camp. We cantered the first four miles, with the Basuto scouts well in front of us. The guide wanted to canter all the way, but I did the rest dismounted, with a few of my men out, preferring caution at night with Boers about. When we got to the junction of the roads we left our horses with a small guard, lined the road the Boers were to come by with twenty rifles in a good place a mile further on, and waited anxiously.

Soon daylight came; no Boers; so we mounted, and leaving word for the Leicesters and 18th Hussars, I pushed on down the road to the drift they were expected by. The Basuto scout came on a Boer track, and went off like a hound on the scent. We followed him right to the *drift* six miles on, where we came on the Boers, over twenty of them, with seven waggons, 450 cattle, fifteen rifles and ammunition, and good trek oxen, six ponies and three mules. They put up a white flag and surrendered when they saw us coming. It was a good haul, because many of them were Natal rebels. They had mealies on their waggons, so we were able to give our horses a good feed; also they had a good supply of matches, which we were very glad of.

The Boers didn't want to move, saying it was Sunday; but I told them they must inspan in an hour, and that they would be just in time for the afternoon service at Piet Retief. On the way back we met Colonel Henry, who had come out with a big force and a pom-pom. He was very pleased to hear of the haul. We came straight back, getting in at 1.30 p.m. after twenty hours on empty stomachs. The colonel and General Smith-Dorrien expressed their satisfaction at our success.

April 1st to 6th.—Escorting convoys to Colonel Allenby's column. A pontoon section R.E. came and bridged the Assegai River at Sandbank, putting the bridge up to the admiration of us all, and the astonishment of the Swazis, in under two hours.

Easter Sunday, April 7th.—The colonel read the service, and after it the latest Reuter telegrams from home—"Twenty-two guns taken since our trek began," "Twenty-four clasps to be given for the South-African medal," "Doyly Carte dead," and one or two other items, showing we were in touch with the outer world. We are tormented by flies here, and long to start anywhere. Lost two more horses from horse-sickness.

Monday and Tuesday, April 8th and 9th.—More convoy work. Swarms of flies, and no news; shall all be glad to move.

Wednesday, April 10th.—At last we leave Sandbank, and, though we don't know where we may go or what is going to happen, the feeling of having one's nose turned towards the line is very satisfactory. The column moved to Piet Retief, where we found a large convoy arriving from Volksrust, miles of waggons making clouds of dust, and with them Legard and his party, who had done very well. Got letters from home, 17th to 23rd February, also some very welcome parcels, especially the soap, which we were out of.

Thursday and Friday, April 11th and 12th—Resting and recouping horses at Piet Retief. The horses are now given fourteen pounds of oats, which is too much. Got all horses re-shod, Farrier-Sergeant Kennedy working very hard. Much speculation as to future plans.

Saturday, April 13th.—Heard we were to trek back to Middelburg, starting next day. Colonel Allenby's column to join ours, the two under Colonel Campbell, which will make us a strong force. The sudden increase of rations has knocked a good many horses up, though we have not given them the whole of it, and have given it in many small feeds. Horses are all very poor. We can only mount sixty men, but that is above the average.

Sunday, April 14th.—Started at 5.30 a.m. from Piet Retief, all of us in great spirits at the prospect of getting back to Middelburg. Colonel Campbell's force with Colonel Allenby's is about 3000 strong, made up as follows:

Scots Greys, 6th Carabineers, 18th Hussars, 100 K.R.R. M.I.—

about 600 mounted men and 300 dismounted under Colonel Allenby, Inniskilling Dragoons.
1st Leicesters and Lancashire Fusiliers—about 1600.
One 5-inchgun, two 15-pounders 21st F.B.R.A. two 12-pounders O Battery R.H.A., one 12-pounder naval gun, one 12-pounder Armstrong gun, one howitzer, two pom-poms—under Major H. Corbyn, R.A.
R.E. telegraph and pontoon sections.
Total, about 3000.

Marched to Idalia, twelve miles north-west of Piet Retief. Greys had one man killed. One has less to do in these large columns, and I think at this stage of the war, when the Boers never make a stand, small columns supporting each other, and always well entrenched at night, would do more good. Every man would then do a share of fighting each day, and the country would be better cleared.

A lot of horses have fever, due to the increase in the ration of oats from two pounds to fourteen pounds a day, this in spite of the fact that we have fed ours five times a day, and not given them the whole. Waggon-loads of oats had to be left and destroyed at Piet Retief, as we had not transport for them.

Monday, April 15th.—A short march but a long day, camped a mile beyond the Shela River, which gave great difficulty to the transport.

Tuesday, April 16th.—Advance guard with the 18th Hussars, who are now commanded by Major Marling, V.C. (an old 60th officer). A long march, over roads difficult for the transport, ending in a very difficult *drift* over the Compies River. The Royal Engineers helped with a bridge. The best place for the officer commanding a column on such occasions is at the *drift* itself, and here Colonel Campbell spent most of the day, and with the help of the Leicester regiment, who were in their best form, all but a few waggons were got over. Our horses are much better now, and we can mount just over seventy men. A little sniping, very few Boers, and an open country.

Tomorrow we begin climbing up to the high *veldt*; expect to come on more Boers, and to find it much colder. I think this column is too big; divide it into three and more damage will be done to the Boers.

Wednesday, April 17th.—A short march round the Spitzkop, a great mountain standing by itself, from which it is possible to signal to Wakkerstroom and Paardekop on the Natal railway line. Camped at Witbank, five miles from our last camp on the Compies River, partly to give General Smith-Dorrien's column time to come up level with us, and partly to signal to the line. On rear guard with my company. Saw from fifty to a hundred Boers eight miles off, moving along the high ground to the left of our convoy, which is three miles long. I expect these will try to delay us tomorrow.

Thursday, April 18th.—They did try—about 500—with a gun and a pom-pom (the Carolina pom-pom). The road up to the high *veldt*, which we had to follow, gave the Boers great advantages, if they really meant to fight But it also had its advantages for us, for it led along up a spur, a sort of buttress to the high veldt, which gave us a series of good positions, easy enough for us to take, so long as the Boers did not occupy the ground to our right front. This they did not do, probably owing to the presence of Smith-Dorrien's column at some distance to our right. Thus, though our road was commanded from the front and from both sides, we were able to advance up the right side of our ridge, and escape untouched a good deal of pom-pom fire from the Boers.

The Scots Greys were advance guard with our company in support. About three miles from camp they came under fire. Our guns soon cleared the way, and we were soon in possession of the first position, about three miles up our spur Then more guns came up—the two long range 12-pounder naval guns, Corbyn's two 15-pounders, the two R-H.A. guns, and two pom-poms, all going against the two Boer guns, which were on a height above us to our left front. Gradually we worked on up our spur, the Greys getting a footing on the top about 11 a.m. The Boer pom-pom, though it must often have had a hot time of it, kept dodging about from place to place, moving whenever we had located it, and letting any target we presented have a belt of its one-pound shells.

The road itself was too exposed for our long line of baggage to come on by, so the Boers had to be cleared right away before the convoy could advance. To do this, the colonel sent the Leicesters half left, covered by the guns, down our spur and then up, straight at the high ridge the Boer guns were on. The mounted troops in the meantime, getting up on to the high *veldt*, turned to their left, and making a wide sweep, drove in the Boer left. Our company got to a high rise in the *veldt*, where we very soon found ourselves dismounted and extended, every man shooting for all he was worth at about two hundred Boers retiring.

The Boers had to retire over very boggy ground in the open, about 1000 yards from us. It must have been an anxious time for some of them. We could see them riding hard, arms, elbows and legs going, but making little progress over the swampy ground, while occasionally a Boer or a horse was knocked over. We alone fired 1600 rounds, and the pom-pom and the Greys, who joined us soon afterwards, fired a good deal too. We had already come a long way out of our course, so we hove to, and came back to where the column was camped six miles off. This fighting took place near the farm of the well-known commandant Tobias Smuts, where on the side of the hill that sportsman has planted a huge "T" in eucalyptus trees. This "T" forms a landmark for many miles around.

Let us hope that someday Tobias may return to finish writing his name on his property, for his name is written in the history of his country as a good specimen of the Boer fighting-general, and one who has "played the game."

We camped at Weltervreden, arriving just as it was getting dark, at 5.15 p.m. The Boers seemed to retire towards Ermelo. We are on the high veldt, which means that we are in an open undulating country, and a very cold one. The ground is very boggy in places, and we must look out that we don't get bogged under fire, like our Boer friends today.

Friday, April 19th.—Only moved five miles, owing to boggy ground, camping at Roodevaal near the Vaal River. Smith-Dorrien's column close to us.

Saturday, April 20th.—On rear guard; only a few Boers, and they contented themselves with sniping at what must have been 4000 yards. The advance guard came on 400 Boers, who retired towards Ermelo. Camped at Kranspan, a ten-miles march.

Sunday, April 21st.—Left about 6.30 a.m. Was on the left flank of the convoy, which trailed out for over three miles. I found my seventy men not one too many. A few snipers gave us some trouble, but Legard, who is quite the "old soldier" now, kept them at a respectful distance. We passed quite close to Ermelo, but I did not enter the town. The rear of our column was shelled from the heights on the south side of the town. We camped three miles north-east of Ermelo.

In the afternoon 150 Boers tried to rush Tafel Kop, an isolated hill overlooking Ermelo, but they were kept off by the rear guard. About 4.30 I got orders to picquet this Tafel Kop with my whole company for the night. Colonel Allenby had just heard that there were a lot of Boers about, and had sent reinforcements there. When I got to the top I found it was a large hill, and that to hold it properly I needed nearer three companies than my fifty men. I got there just as it was getting dark, short of tools and time to entrench; very hard ground, and two Boer *laagers* as near me as was our own camp.

The more I looked at it the less I liked it. We dug two circular trenches as best we could, and tying our horses to some trees in the centre, got every man available for defence. If the Boers had meant to have the hill, fifty men could not have prevented them. However, no Boers came, and at dawn when we crept forward to the edges of the hill, I was relieved to find there was no immediate intention of attacking us. A few snipers kept us busy from daylight, but it was not till about 7 a.m. that the Boers began to show in any numbers. About fifty with a pom-pom were working round our right, while about ten snipers bothered us on our left. We could see many Boers in the town of Ermelo.

In daylight, as long as we were on our hill, though rather scattered, we were right enough, but I got uneasy about being cut off in our retirement. The column had started, and it was late when I succeeded in getting orders to retire from the officer commanding the rear guard. We had a three-mile gallop, sections covering each other, and one or two awkward accidents in the shape of falls and broken girths, but we succeeded without loss in retiring through the Boers to the Greys, who were very soon themselves hard pressed. These might have got into serious difficulties but for Major Corbyn's magnificent shooting with the 2 1st Battery.

We covered the retirement of the Greys, and I got a chance of trying my new Mauser pistol at 250 yards. It got jammed when I needed it most, but this was owing to my inexperience. All this time the Boer gun and pom-pom were making good shots at our guns, but luckily did no damage. The Boers kept pushing on with great boldness, about 1000 of them. In the end Major Corbyn gave them such a dose of shrapnel that they left us alone, and we got into camp unmolested for the last five miles, at 3.30 p.m., near Klipstapel. The advance guard had hustled the Boers in their front well. On the whole we have given as good as we got today I expect. Our horses have been saddled-up for thirty-two hours; if they are half as tired as I am, they will sleep well tonight.

Tuesday, April 23rd.—On rear guard again; only a few Boers, and they not very enterprising. The Lancashire Fusiliers got behind, and we helped them on with our horses. The men had never been on a horse before, and thought it a good joke, but it would not have been so amusing if it had happened the day before. Six snipers rode along with us away to our left; otherwise the country, which we could see for miles, seemed to be deserted. Camped at Boshman's Kop, at the head of the Klein Olifants River and Vaal Water.

Wednesday, April 24th.—Marched to Vaalbank, ten miles down the Klein Olifants River. A sergeant-major of the Royal Engineers was shot dead when out foraging at a farm. An easy day for our horses. The Boers are reported to intend attacking our camp at night, but we have the usual circle of trenches round it, and I do not expect they will. We have thirty of our men on night-picquet.

Thursday, April 25th.—A long march to Pullen's Hope. The Royal Engineers put two bridges across the Klein Olifants River. We passed near Reade's grave. I sent my camera to Legard on the left flank, who took two photographs of it. Faulkner came later with the main body and his Cape cart, and was able to plant three small trees which he got from Morrison's Store; he also put a fence round the grave. Legard had a bit of trouble with some snipers to his left. At Pullen's Hope we saw about 150 Boers on the move, but did not go after them. I visited a farm with women and children, and while talking to them got shot at.

Friday, April 26th.—Marched to Eikeboom, only twelve miles from Middelburg. We were rear guard again with the 18th Hussars, who had two horses hit All very glad at the prospect of getting back to the line.

Saturday, April 27th.— We reached Middelburg about noon, and were met by our band, also by Rudolf Jelf, whom I had not seen since Talana, and many others of the battalion. The troops gave the colonel a tremendous ovation as they passed him, for there never was a more popular officer. I heard I had been promoted captain after nine years' service. The colonel had been promoted and made A.D.C. to the king.

FAREWELL ORDER BY COLONEL CAMPBELL TO HIS COLUMN.

After concluding a long and pleasant trek, Lieut.-Colonel

Campbell feels that he cannot sufficiently thank the Staff, 18th Hussars, R.A., M.I., and 1st Leicesters for the ready, willing, and excellent manner in which they have severally carried out their duties whilst under his command. He specially mentions Major Laming, 18th Hussars, and the mounted troops, who were always ready to turn out for anything at any moment, and their scouting was admirable. Lieut.-Colonel Campbell hopes that someday all these units may again be under his command, and wishes them all good luck.

PART 6

Lydenburg, April 28th to October 12th, 1901

We were indeed glad to return to the civilisation of Middelburg after three months' continual trekking, and thoroughly enjoyed the comforts of a standing camp, with its tents, field-force canteen, letters, papers, news, bread, etc., to say nothing of respite from the reports of guns and Mausers, and from being constantly on the alert There were many other columns at Middelburg, just returned from most successful operations to the north of the line, and one seemed to see or hear of every friend one had ever known. There was much news to exchange. Things seemed to be going well everywhere, and the end appeared to be in sight.

We got busy at once, refitting and re-horsing, for what some thought was to be the final move against the Boers. Our one hope was that we should be left with Colonel Campbell's column, for however much we had "groused" at the continual rain, and however sick we had at times felt of the war, we had, even at the darkest moments, realised that we were extremely well off. But the hope which Colonel Campbell had expressed, that "all the units would again serve under his command," was not to be fulfilled, for on May 2nd my Company got sudden orders to move to Lydenburg to do garrison duty, and, starting next day with Lynes and R. Seymour, arrived there about May 10th. I myself got leave to go to Pretoria, where I drew stores and equipment for my company, and the dentist drew four teeth for me.

Being unable to get a convoy up to Lydenburg from Machadodorp, I spent some time between Pretoria, Middelburg, and Machadodorp, collecting stores and horses, and on May 23rd I got twenty volunteers of the Special Service Volunteer Company K.R.R. under Captain

Coakley. These men we fitted out with horses and equipment and took to Machadodorp, where we spent the time of waiting for a convoy in training them in riding and M.I. duties. They had come from various London Volunteer battalions at a time when men were badly wanted, and brought an infusion of keenness which had a good effect. They were good shots, too, and picked up the work quickly. Some found the work harder and less glorious than they had expected, but the majority stuck to it well, and the fact that they had seven casualties before they left shows how well they did their share.

The 2nd of June found us still at Machadodorp waiting for a convoy, It was the coldest day I remember "ever or anywhere." There were many columns trekking on the high veldt to the south of the railway line at this time, and I expect many who were with them will remember the cold of that day. We had all expected great things from these columns, but something seemed to have gone wrong somewhere. We got no news, and they got no Boers.

Friday, June 7th.—We started with a large convoy and a fair escort to join the company up at Lydenburg. The customary rumour that Ben Viljoen was going to attack our convoy in the Badfontein Valley, seemed more probable than usual, so that the precaution was taken of sending Colonel Benson's column up at the same time.

We arrived at Lydenburg on the 11th, my detachment of volunteers marching in with all the appearance of old mounted infantry hands, well turned out and in every way a credit to the company. Unfortunately I got malaria in the Badfontein Valley, and had to go to hospital on my arrival at Lydenburg. The fever developed into jaundice, which laid me up for ten days. This complete rest, after a year's hard work without a pause, did me good, so that on the 23rd, when I came off the sick list, I was all the better able to take over the company and resume work.

Sunday, June 23rd.—I found the company was getting hard work, and work of a most trying kind, for the garrison was small, and the precautions taken against attack were extreme. Besides the day-picquets, grazing-guards, escorts to convoys and fatigues on the defences, half our men and an officer were on picquet each night. By day a picquet would be sniped, or a stray cow driven off by a Boer, and the whole company turned out; by night a shot from some sniping Boer or jumpy sentry frequently turned the whole garrison out. There was all the hard work and risk of being with a column in the field, with none of the chances of getting your own back. No wonder I found the company longing to get back to Colonel Campbell.

During my absence one man. Private Redmond, had been killed by a Boer sniper while watering his horse; another man had had three bullets through his clothes without being hit.

Wednesday, July 2nd.—We got orders to trek with Colonel Park's column, which was at Lydenburg. We left at 2 a.m. on the 3rd, a cold moonlight night, with two days' rations—my company 115 strong, but very badly off for boots, which we had been unable to obtain. The scheme, which was to have given us Commandant Moll and 200 Boers fell through, because the Boers got warning of our intentions; so that when we reached Kruger's Post we found the place empty. There was a little sniping, but the Boers in these parts are poor fighters compared to those of Carolina and Ermelo, We brought in the wife of President Schalk Burgers, and returned on the 4th, our only causalities being three horses hit.

Saturday, July 5th.—Lynes, Coakley, and fifty men again left with Colonel Park's Column on a nine days' trek, returning on the 14th, having accomplished little owing to the difficulties of the country.

The chief recommendation of Lydenburg was its excellent polo ground, made by the Rifle Brigade in 1900, and when possible we used to play three days a week, This, and the arrival of convoys with mails, about once in three weeks, and an occasional night sitting up for Boers, were our chief interests. It is a nice enough place in itself, but we were cut off from the world; we were doing the drudgery of the campaign, and longed to get away; so that when a call was made for volunteers for a corps of M.I. scouts, which was being formed at Middleburg, I volunteered with most of my company.

About this time the plan of getting four M.I. companies of the regiment together, was beginning to take shape, so that I was not altogether disappointed when we heard that the scheme of M.I. Scouts had fallen through.

Friday, July 25th.—We got orders to hand over forty-three of our horses to the Liverpool Company of M.I. We had taken great trouble with our horses and much regretted this order, for the loss of the horses, besides being discouraging, meant that we could only find small escorts to the convoys—often, in my opinion, too small for safety.

Tuesday, August 13th.—The second week in August the local Boers, who had been very quiet of late, began to get more active. On the 13th we suffered a sad loss. At 7.30 a.m. Corporal Casey galloped in and reported that three men of one of our picquets, two miles east of the town, had been killed. This post had been chosen with much care. It was a difficult one to approach, but a picquet, once there, had an excellent position. The men had perhaps got over-confident from having gone some time without seeing a Boer, though they seemed to have taken the precautions ordered, "Be careful how you go out" were the last words said to them by Sergeant-Major Rowat as they left the lines that morning at 6.30 a.m. At 5.30 p.m. we had buried three of them.

The custom was for twelve men to go out to this post, six of them returning as soon as they had seen the picquet safely posted. On this occasion there was a high wind, and it seems that Humphries, Hawken, and Graham did not allow time enough for the flankers to get round. They dismounted, and walked through the rocks and long grass into an ambush. Though a dozen shots were fired, not one was heard by the rest of the party, owing to the wind.

When we arrived on the scene, Humphries and Hawken were lying dead in shooting positions, their rifles discharged, and Graham died very shortly afterwards in great pain. The Boers had only time to take the horses. Expanding bullets had been used. This loss of three very good men in such a way went as near raising ill-feeling between Briton and Boer as I have at any time seen during the war.

The next morning I went out with the picquet in force, and found about twenty Boers there, but they left in a hurry. We set fire to all the long grass, thinking it better that the cattle should go without than we should lose any more men in this Whitechapel way.

Monday, August 19th.—I left with twelve men for Middelburg to try and get horses, of which we were getting very short. Arriving at Middelburg on the 24th, and finding that they would give no horses to troops on lines of communication, I went on to Pretoria, which I reached on the 25th.

Travelling on the railway was much safer than it had been. At Uitkyk, the place with such a bad name nine months before, there was a small fort and garrison, the officers of which were playing golf. There were blockhouses all along the line, absolutely safe from rifle-fire, and surrounded by a network of wire. All the men had to do was to be alert. At one blockhouse, the scene of my adventure with the commander-in-chief's train, there were half-a-dozen men playing football. I thought to myself, "You wouldn't have done that six months ago, my boys!"

In Pretoria I saw many of those in authority, but could get no horses. The chances of our battalion of M.I. being formed seemed very hopeful. I lost two more teeth, which made a total of eight pulled out during the war. It was some consolation to feel that there were eight less to have toothache in, but the problem of how to negotiate the ration biscuit was becoming a difficult one.

Returning to Middelburg, I managed, by asking till I became a nuisance, to get fifteen out of the fifty horses required, and left Machadodorp with Watson, who had come to join us, with a convoy on September 6th. The escort to this convoy was weaker than usual, and rumours were consequently stronger that we should be attacked in the Badfontein Valley. An attack seemed so probable that we stood by for a day at Shoeman's Kloof, awaiting reinforcements. Eventually we got to Lydenburg on September 9th without seeing a Boer.

The month of September dragged on, and the war seemed to make little progress. We at Lydenburg were constantly worried with rumours that Ben Viljoen, a specialist in night-attacks, was going to try us. Picquets were doubled and escort duties grew heavier. We longed for Ben to attack but he never came.

The rains began, and spring was coming on, the burned *veldt* began to get green; flowers, vegetables, and trees were coming to life, and Lydenburg was getting more beautiful each day. But with the return of spring the war was getting a new lease of life, and we knew that it must go on till at least next cold weather.

At the end of September, by way of diversion, we held some successful sports. All the people of Lydenburg were present, and many gave prizes for events.

In October, Eustace moved down to Middelburg to start a *depôt* for the 25th K.R.R. M.I., which was now (on paper at least) a *fait accompli*. On the 7th two of our 4th Battalion Companies M.I., under Hope and Dalby, came into Lydenburg, having had some difficult fighting and a good many causalities with Colonel Park to the north of Lydenburg.

PART 7

Colonel Benson's Column

On 12th October we got a wire saying K.R.R. M.I. were to concentrate at Middelburg to join Colonel Benson's column. This was the best news I could have had for my birthday, as I had felt the four months' drudgery at Lydenburg very much. We moved off at 12 next day with an ox convoy and all our kit, doing double marches and killing thirty oxen, and reached Machadodorp in three days, and Middelburg in three more. The weather was glorious, and the fact of having three of our own companies collected together for the first time, combined to make it an enjoyable march. Very little time at Middelburg on 18th to get everything done, but now we are all more or less ready, the company as strong and as well turned out as I have seen it in the five years I have known it.

The company is three officers and 130 men strong; the battalion, under Eustace, 350 strong. The column, about 2000 strong, is composed of three squadrons of Scottish Horse, 3rd M.I., the Buffs, four guns of the 84th Battery, and two pom-poms. Printed standing orders in this column, and everything much stricter; still, if we know what is wanted, we shall get on all right.

Sunday, October 20th.—Celebrated Talana day by starting our trek with Benson's column and the First Regimental Battalion M.I. ever formed. Did fifteen miles to Driefontein south-west of Middelburg. Left at 6, got in at 12, and dined with Murray (Black Watch), who was at Talana on General Symonds' staff, and is now in command of the 2nd Scottish Horse.

Monday, October 21st.—Stayed at Driefontein, collecting information, a busy day for us, as we found all picquets—five posts three miles out, and two night-posts. Went to a farm with Reggie Seymour and got twelve very wild chickens. Several Boers in distance, about four miles south-west. Posted two night-picquets.

Tuesday, October 22nd,—Colonel Benson having gone on over night with 3rd M.I. and Scottish Horse, we came on with convoy seven miles to junction of Olifants River and Steenkool Spruit. Was on left with three sections. Got in about 11. Colonel Benson got in about 1 p.m., having caught thirty-seven Boers, cattle and sheep.

His system of information under Wools Sampson is splendid, and he acts on it, which is the secret of his success. The Boers call him "the mad Englishman," and say there is nothing simpler for them than to dodge other columns, but Benson's column frightens them, and they won't sleep within thirty miles of it knowingly.

A terrible storm about 4 p.m., hailstones as big as racquet balls, stampeded all the horses; luckily all ours were knee-haltered and grazing near us, so we got them all back. The other corps lost about 100 between them. A wet night made things very uncomfortable, most of the tents and shelters having been blown down.

Wednesday, October 23rd.—Went out north-east with company and Scottish Horse in search of stampeded horses, as far as last camp. Got nine horses and caught one Boer, seeing two more. We ought to have got all three Boers, but scouts went wrong. It cleared up in afternoon and gave us a chance of getting dry.

Thursday, October 24th.—An easy day. At 5 p.m. got notice of a night march, baggage and infantry to come on next morning to Rietkail, seventeen miles south-west. Left at 6.30 p.m. A clear moonlight night. The idea was to round up 200 Boers, said to be twenty miles off. Marched all night, mostly at a walk, with occasional halts and leads. Moved in sections, undulating over the *veldt* and avoiding sky lines. At 1.30 we halted, and those who were not too cold, slept, while our native scouts went on. About 3 a.m. we pushed on again, and as day dawned about 4 a.m. we broke into a trot; then, forming a long line— one company K.R.R., one 3rd M.I., and one Scottish Horse, with remainder of corps in support—we galloped on about five miles, but the Boers had heard of our coming, and cleared.

The Scottish Horse came on them in distance, but, thinking they were our own people, left them alone till too late. It was a long gallop after a long march, but our horses, with exception of two or three, kept up well. I did not quite like the risk of letting men get out of hand till I could see what was on. The 200 Boers were there right enough, but we did not get to close quarters. We had a few causalities, including our doctor killed (Robertson), only just arrived in the country, poor chap. We halted till about 8 a.m. at a farm (Witbank) eight miles from our new camp.

We could see the Boers waiting and watching on high ground about four miles off. I felt pretty sure they would bother the rear guard, so when we were told off for that duty I knew the K.R.R. M.I. were going to be tested. My company and Lynes' were the two rearmost companies. The moment the guns left, the Boers came on at a gallop, our men and horses coming under fire from the very first. Not to make a long story of it, we kept on retiring and holding positions, while the Boers thrust right gallantly, some firing at us, while more kept working round. Our men did splendidly, the chief difficulty being to get them to retire when one wanted them to. In these shows it is the getting away that one must attend to as much as the fighting; I should often have liked to hang on.

The Boers were coming right on in the open, sometimes only 250 yards off, so that then we had the advantage; but their turn always came when we retired, and we had many exciting retirements. Our luck was very good, we only lost eight horses, and had one man hit in two places, but not seriously (Allen—this is the third man of the name in my Company we have had hit). Unfortunately Bircham's 4th Battalion Company got into difficulties, and had Troyte and Crichton wounded. Troyte was left out with three men in the hands of the Boers, so that we don't yet know if it is a bad wound. This Boer commando seems to be under Groeblar, Erasmus, and Trichard. They had collected with a view to making a night-attack on Benson's column, which had been causing them great annoyance.

We both were on our way to attack each other, and our *Kaffir* scouts met about twelve miles from camp. Whoever they were, they came on against superior numbers, and in the open, with great boldness. Both Murray, who went right through on the Natal side, and Colonel Benson, who has been through everything since Magersfontein, agreed that they had never seen them so bold. Colonel Benson was much pleased with the way our men did, and several complimentary remarks were made. Got back to camp about 5 p.m. very tired after a long outing. Slept jolly well.

Saturday, October 26th.—A welcome day of sunshine and rest. Hear Troyte is being well looked after by Boers. Boers say they had a bad time of it yesterday.

Sunday, October 27th.—An early start. Took right flank with half company, Seymour and Watson on left flank of second line (ox-transport, which left 4.30.) Whole first line left 5.30. A few Boers on my right, but they kept a long way off. We camped at Kaffirstad, which found us on the flank at a farm full of geese and chickens, which we cleared. On getting into camp at 12, heard Seymour had had a nasty time, his scouts just saving him from a very clever ambush. Poor Egan, one of my best men, shot through liver, and three horses shot. All seem to have done very well, especially Seymour, Corporal Brindley, and Egan, who, when his horse was killed and himself shot, stuck to his rifle and ran back 100 yards to warn them, In afternoon went out farm-clearing, so we had a long day. Went to see Egan who was very bad, but quite plucky. Told him he had saved his section. He said, "Someone must stop the bullets." This is the second time he has been hit. We are on rear guard tomorrow and are certain to be worried,

Monday, October 28th.—Left Rietkail camp at 4. 15 a.m. to relieve outposts. At first it was very difficult to see what the direction of the next march was to be. We were spread out over nearly five miles, and I had a lot of hard work in getting all my men in right positions, and making it clear to each when and how to retire, all the more as there was a difficult *spruit* to be crossed and I was not very clear myself There were Boers visible from all my posts, but luckily they did not press on much at first A delay from a waggon breaking down might have been a bore. Three miles on we got stopped in a fairly good position, as the waggons were sticking at a difficult *drift*. A lot of Boers came on on our left flank (my right rear).

We had to hold on a long time, and some of the firing was at pretty close quarters. We were lucky again, and got away with only one horse hit. There were said to be quite 200 under Groebelar. I only saw about seventy myself; a few followed us right up, but the rest went off towards Bethel. I am quite sure the only way to cope with them is to have a lot of columns under one good man, and to work them into a corner of blockhouses.

Got into camp about 3 p.m., a bit tired; heard poor Egan was dead; chose a place for grave and made a sketch to mark the spot. Had to read the service myself. Poor Egan, he was one of my best men, and when one looked at him one knew he would do a lot for one.

Tuesday, October 29th.—Remained in camp here, and was glad of the rest Some of our horses are done up, and all the men have had hard work. This morning firing began early, 5.30; the day-picquets found by 3rd M.I., having two men hit and two taken. Boers had to be driven off by 3rd M.I., who saw about 200, evidently intending to follow us up.

Thursday, October 31st,—The ox-convoy under Eustace left Sieferfontein camp at 4.30 a.m., a place about forty miles south of Brug Spruit, on east railway line, and about thirty-five miles north-east of Standerton on Natal line. Lynes' company and Bircham's, three companies Buffs, two guns 84th Battery, and a pom-pom as escort. The intended march was to Onderwacht, twelve miles due north. At 5.30 a.m. the remainder of the convoy, under Colonel Benson, left, with 3rd M.I., two guns and pom-pom as rear guard, the remainder, Scottish Horse, Buffs, and two K.R.R. companies M.I., were with the convoy as escort and on flanks. Our two companies were in advance of the one convoy, and in rear of the other. The second convoy overtook the first at a bad *drift* two-and-a-half-miles after starting, so that my company was in the centre. We had no particular orders, but were available where required.

Our rear guard and its pom-pom were very soon at work; at 5 a.m. they were shooting, and there were evidently plenty of Boers in that direction. When we had gone about two-and-a-half miles I could see there was something going on on our right flank about two miles out. Both the right flank guards of the two convoys were doing a bit of shooting and a lot of galloping about The high ridge they were on was about two miles to our right, and was one of those which it is so difficult to know whether to hold or not In this case it was held, but weakly.

I said, "Surely those are Boers," but Watson and Sergeant Rowat did not think so; it was quite impossible to say for certain. Presently there was a good deal of shooting, and the right flank guard of the first convoy came galloping in to the advance guard. One of my signallers, who had been attached to Bircham on the right flank, came up and rather excitedly told me that Bircham had been wounded and his section driven in by the Boers, who were right up to him. I had no orders from anyone, so I sent Watson up to Eustace with half a company to report to him, telling him at the same time that I had no orders from Benson to do so. I let Colonel Benson know at the same time.

Just about this time (7 a.m.) rain and very cold wind came on, and there was a thick mist. They were shooting on three sides, and it was altogether unpleasant. I went up to see Eustace to try to find out what was going on, and found him as much in the dark as myself. He asked me to go and reinforce a height on our left, on which they seemed to be hesitating, and which it was important to hold, as the convoy was parked below it I was to try and find out what was going on and let Eustace know.

When I got there, dismounting most of the men to hold the hill, I pushed on with a few scouts and found the hill all clear, but saw about 160 Boers moving slowly and unconcernedly away in two clumps about one mile off. This was, as I found out afterwards, the same party we had seen earlier, two miles to our right They had swooped down in the mist, collared a few of Lynes' scouts, and were now on our left. They were mostly dressed in cavalry cloaks and slouch hats, and got right up, shouting "Stop!" before the mistake was seen. Eyre, whose section got cut off, had a narrow escape himself, while his horse was shot. Lynes, who did well, got his men back to a farm, which he held and shot from. His horse was killed, shot in two places, and he himself hit on the knuckles.

Soon after I got up, Colonel Benson, who was always where there was any shooting, came up with a pom-pom, I told him what had happened. There was no doubt now that there were a great many Boers all round us. There was a thick mist, and the waggons were getting bogged at the *drift* behind us. It was a difficult position, but it did not seem to worry Colonel Benson in the least, He halted on the high ground and got his waggons together, while we all waited and got very cold and wet. When we did advance the infantry went out in front, while the mounted troops were drawn in.

The rear guard under Major Anley, Essex Regiment, was doing a lot of shooting, having to wait for two bogged waggons. They must have been having a nasty time of it.

About 11 a.m. it began to clear. About three miles from the *drift*, six from the start, the Scottish Horse were sent to help the rear guard, and three of my sections sent to support the advance guard, while my No. 1 section was left as escort to the guns. About a mile on I saw some of Lynes' men in front of me dismount and shoot from a ridge, so I galloped at once with a section, and coming up on their right we were in time to receive and give back a few long-range shots at about sixty Boers who were retiring in the open.

We were now on the hill, which was destined to become a very warm spot, and the scene of the hardest fighting on both sides that I have seen this war. At the time of our arrival on this spot, about noon, it was the position of the left of the advance guard. Eventually at sunset, which still found us there, it had become the right rear of the column, and three thousand yards away.

Eustace came up soon after I had got there and said, "We are going to camp somewhere near here. You are to hold this hill, while I take Lynes on the hill to the right, beyond." He left one gun with me, with orders for it to wait till relieved by the other two in the rear. Luckily it did not do so. There was on the top of this hill a cup-shaped hollow, with a grand view to the front and a fair view to the rear, an ideal position for one of the picquets round the camp, which we should, in the ordinary course of events, have had to find. We made a note of this at the time.

The Boers to our front had cleared away some distance, but, looking to our rear, I saw there was something important going on, what it was it was impossible to make out. Facing the rear—one-and-a-half miles half-right (*i.e.* on left flank of the column)—there were over 300 mounted men making slowly to a farm. I rushed to the gun and told the sergeant to shoot, which he did, the shell falling just beyond the farm. Then I saw what were certainly some of our men, further from the column than those I had fired at; so, thinking I had made a mistake in firing, I told the sergeant to stop. There was the greatest difficulty throughout the day in distinguishing our men from Boers, and this difficulty was greatly increased by the use of these beastly slouch hats and black overcoats.

Suddenly there was very heavy firing in the rear. The 300 mounted men at the farm shot out and extended at a very fast gallop, joining hands with about 700 mounted men to the rear, all shouting, shooting, and thrusting. There must have been 1000 of the finest Boers in the country charging the rear guard. Soon I saw this flood mix with the infantry and come right on and on up to the two guns, a mile in the rear and below me. My gun kept firing away, but seeing the flood still coming on I sent it away, and lined out my men in the best positions available, pointing out what to fire at, and telling them we must hold our hill. There were, besides the hollow before mentioned, one or two good places of the same kind, though smaller. Wonderfully soon we were under a heavy fire ourselves, and shooting back steadily and hard. It did one good to see how steady the men were.

The Boers, who had originally retired in front of us, were now coming back, so on three sides of us there were Boers. I joined Watson, Sergeant-Major Rowat, and five men in the hollow before alluded to. Quoting Lychenburg, of the 18th Hussars, I said, "Now, men, we are in a jolly tight hole, but a jolly good hole, and we are going to make the most of it." I should say this was about 12.30 p.m. We shot a lot at first, but very soon the Boers got our range, and shooting became dangerous.

Very soon, to my awful grief, the sergeant-major—poor Rowat, the best N.C.O. in the army—fell back, hit through the head and apparently done for. While we were attending to him several shots came right in, and we had to keep down, taking careful stealthy shots at the heads we could only occasionally see on a ridge about 250 yards off and slightly below us. Soon Cherriman was hit in three places. Curiously enough this man was hit the same day two years ago at Lombard's Kop. None of these were dangerous wounds.

Livesay, my late servant, did splendidly, shooting back and talking to the Boers he was shooting at—"Would you?" "I see you my friend," "Take that," and such like comments. About an hour after we began reinforcements came up, Seymour bringing up some more of the company. Right well they faced the bullets, and it was here that we lost poor Sergeant Wayman and Corporal Brindley, and other very valuable lives. Three companies of the Buffs also came up, but having fifteen casualties they retired, and thus forced some of my men, who had no cover, also to retire.

Reggie Seymour, B. Seymour, and three men joined us in our hollow. There was hardly room for us all now, but we were glad of their ammunition. Very soon poor Reggie and Corporal Oglesby were hit. We cut Seymour's coats open (I never saw a fellow with so many clothes on), and were relieved to find it was a clean wound—arm broken, same place as mine, but a clean wound. Livesay set the arm very well with two scabbards. All this time we kept up an occasional shot and accounted for a horse or a Boer.

The time went quickly, but the ammunition went quicker, and after two hours or so it began to give out. We had been throwing what we could spare, tied up in handkerchiefs, to a party close to us. About this time Casey, Pedrick, and Baker came up with ammunition, the two former flat on their stomachs. Casey came right in to us; the others lay very flat under the crest. Baker came up at a run in the open and drew a very hot fire, dropping flat, killed as I thought at the time, beside Corporal Rowles, who was under a bit of cover six yards away.

We had lots of ammunition now. At one time it looked as if the Boers were retiring, and we fired more and with less caution, but we soon found there were some excellent marksmen still on the ridge, so resuming our former tactics we kept down and fired more carefully. The Boers kept coming back in twos and threes. We thought they must just have gone to get more ammunition, but heard later that it was Louis Botha with a *sjambok* who kept sending them back. We must have hit some of these. There was soon a large number of Boers collected on the old ridge, and we again had to lie very doggo. The incessant crack of their rifles was very loud, and at times it was difficult to believe they were not within twenty yards of us.

About this time our guns from camp opened fire on the ridge the Boers were on. But to our horror our own pom-pom and a captured gun, dropped shells very near us. One shell in our little cockpit would have sent all fourteen to glory, I sent Pedrick, who was still lying about twenty yards off under the ridge, to crawl back and tell them that it was us they were turning the pom-pom on to. Later I sent Corporal Rowles back from his place to say that I could hang on, but wanted food, ammunition, and water, and that there were quite enough Boers to rush us if they tried it; also that I had four wounded. While they were away the pom-pom placed four shells just to our left, then four just to the right, and then a lot in the middle. There was a groan from the good Livesay, and he fell back with a lot of blood about the head.

I got a field-dressings and to my great relief found it was only three splinters, and that the wounds were not bad. I tied him up, so now we had five out of action. There were still R. Seymour, Watson, five men, and myself. We began burrowing with swords. I feared a shell, but said to myself, "If it does come it will be fate, and it can't be helped."

We afterwards found that our camp was 3000 yards off, and it was impossible for them to see us. We were isolated, and it was getting dark. We had been in our cockpit on the top of the hill the whole afternoon, and the Boers, who evidently wanted the hill, were collecting in good numbers. There were over 300 of them within 300 yards of us, and I was sure they would rush us at dark. I gave out that we would let them come right on up to within six yards and shoot as many as we could. I had two rifles, one carbine, and my Mauser pistol, all full cock and loaded, so that I could not complain of my battery.

At this crisis Pedrick got back to his old place and shouted, "Major Eustace says you are to retire at once, and he will cover you with the guns." At first we were against leaving the wounded, but remembering that Eustace knew they were there when he sent us the order, we decided to try it

Now retiring was no easy matter. We had to come out of our cockpit, and however flat we crawled we were bound to be shot at. The first three got away unnoticed, probably owing to the failing light We said goodbye to Seymour and others, and then took our turn. I crawled out flatter than any pancake, and wriggled along at a great pace, bullets spattering round me. Just behind I heard a cry, and looking round saw poor Scrimshaw bowled over. Watson got up and ran, and I said to myself, "If a long-legged chap like that don't get hit, why should I"—so I got up and ran like the wind, with *'crack' 'crack'* all round me, I was delighted to find all the party, except Scrimshaw and two others cut off beyond us, were safe.

The Boers, when they saw what we were up to, had stood up and fired, any number of them. Seymour told me later they were on him almost immediately we left. We had taken all the bolts of our rifles and the remaining ammunition with us, so we did not leave them much. But unfortunately I left my helmet and pipe, which I have had all through the war, also my haversack with my notes on rear guards. Louis Botha will smile when he sees them. He has taught us something of rear guards today.

It was dark when we got into camp. We put the ambulance on to the wounded, who got in about 2 p.m. When we got in we heard for the first time that it was Louis Botha and over 1500 men we had been competing with; also that Benson, Murray, Lindsay, Guiness, Lloyd, and many others were killed. Sergeants Ashfield and Wayman, Corporal Brindley, and seven of my good fellows all killed, and many more wounded, besides two guns taken. The news about the general had reached us when we got our ammunition. It was a terrible day, and on top of it Louis Botha was expected to attack us that night and follow up his success. A terrible storm came on, it was cold and wet, but we had no time to be depressed.

Myself, somehow, except for my anxiety about Rowat, I felt easy in mind, and I felt sure that the white heather which had seen me through the day would see us through the night too. I was told to get my men out as soon as possible, and get them into *sangars*, which natives and *coolies* and the earlier arrivals in camp had been building. It was pitch dark and stormy; our post was the furthest away and nearest the Boers. No one quite knew where it was. We (forty men) slushed our way out, cold and wretched, about one-and-a-quarter miles, and after various enquiries at other posts, some of whom were afraid to speak above a whisper for fear of drawing fire, we found Corporal Thompson with about thirty of our men. There were only two small works dug, and no tools available, so I was very much annoyed; and leaving Watson in charge of Corporal Thompson's thirty, I brought all my forty back to the camp, turning into my bivouac to avoid the storm till the moon should be up.

About 9.30 it cleared up, and the moon gave a good light, by which I was able to find four spades. With these we worked in reliefs the whole night, and by dawn had good cover for forty men. About an hour after dawn I got an order that the top of the hill must be held, and I was to go at once and entrench. This, after our exertions, was a bit sickening, and simply could not have been done if the Boers had been on the ridge beyond, as reported. However, we set to work with a will, and by 9 a.m. we had a splendid trench—a regular fort. Luckily the Boers, as at Ingogo in 1880, had missed their chance. We heard afterwards that Louis Botha did collect 1400 men for a night-attack, but at 3 a.m. they changed their minds.

We were by 10 a.m. ready for anyone, and hoped they would come. Colonel Wools Sampson had assumed command, and was much pleased with the way our fellows had dug. The Boers were said to be only four miles off, but I could see none—very different from yesterday.

The whole of the 31st the column lay low—it was like a man staggered by a blow. It was by no means beaten, it was ready to fight again, yet it was glad of a pause for breath.

When we looked round we realised what a heavy blow it had been. As I mentioned above. Colonel Benson—one of the most brilliant leaders the war had produced—was dead, together with the others named. The casualties had amounted to 280, besides the loss of those two guns.

The three officers of the Yorkshire Light Infantry M.I. and most of the company had been wiped out, and the Scottish Horse had lost almost as heavily. In my company one officer, four out of five sergeants, six corporals, and thirteen men had been hit—in all ten killed and fourteen wounded. Of the gallant Sergeant Ashfield's section, which had been left as escort to the guns, only three men escaped, and those three, who were holding the horses, had to be ordered back twice by a staff officer before they would leave their comrades. The other three sections had all lost their section-sergeants and many grand men besides.

The loss of a man like Sergeant Rowat, which we all feared, filled us with anxiety. The crowded hospital that day was a sad sight, and the doctors had more work than they could do. Many men died of their wounds, and among them we buried, near Colonel Benson at the farm, Private Tew, a good soldier. We had also lost our Company waggon with blankets and many important documents.

The day passed quietly—fatigue parties went out to bury the dead, and Boers were only seen at a distance. At night we were ready and alert in our *sangars*, but except for heavy firing from some of the infantry posts there was nothing to disturb us,

Friday, November 1st.—With October our anxieties ended. Scouts went out and found that Louis Botha had retired towards Ermelo. The country for miles was clear of Boers. About noon heliographs flashed to us from three different directions.

We had been relieved by Allenby, the ubiquitous De Lisle, and Colonel Barter—each of these columns had made splendid marches to help us, Sergeant-Major Rowat made a great improvement, and our Company waggon with most of the documents was recovered.

Saturday, November 2nd.—The next day we sent all our wounded with Colonel Barter's column to Springs, and our column, under Colonel Wools Sampson, trekked back to Brug Spruit, on the Eastern Railway, arriving there on the 5th.

Having had further trouble with my teeth, I got a day's leave, and riding in with the advanced scouts of the advance guard, arrived just in time to jump into a train for Pretoria, where I enjoyed for twenty-four hours the civilisation of Spruit's Hotel, and returned to Brug Spruit next night.

Part 8

Colonel Mackenzie's Column

The great blow, so suddenly and skilfully delivered by the Boers at Baakenlaagte, would in any of our small wars have been looked upon as a national calamity, but in a war on so large a scale as this one it was merely an incident After five very busy days spent in refitting, time was called, and the column, which had scarcely recovered from the shock, was, without so much as a pat on the back, again dispatched, into the arena. It was this time commanded by Colonel Colin Mackenzie with a new staff.

The two lost guns were replaced by two 12-pounders of longer range, and the place of the Buffs was taken by the Royal Scots Fusiliers. The rest were as before, except that Major Bramley, of the 19th Hussars, took command of the Scottish Horse, while they and the 3rd M.I. and we ourselves started with reduced numbers and much handicapped by losses in officers and N.CO.'s.

The full diary which I kept during the next three months of the wanderings of this column by day and night might convey some idea of the monotony and worries of this stage of the war. But I should be sorry to inflict on anyone a fraction of the boredom which we ourselves went through, so I will only record briefly the chief events.

During the night of November 11th there was a heavy thunderstorm at Brug Spruit, and three men of the Cameron Highlanders were killed by lightning in their tent On the 12th we left Brug Spruit with General Bruce Hamilton, who had taken over the command of the seven columns which were to operate in the Eastern Transvaal. Moving to Bombardy, twenty two miles south-south-west of Brug Spruit, and not far from Baakenlaagte, we waited there until the 18th, covering the advance of the S.A.C. blockhouse line, which ran north and south from the Eastern to the Natal railway.

During this halt I took 150 men over to Baakenlaagte for the purpose of communicating by heliograph with other columns. We started at 3.30 a.m., and got into communication with Colonel Allenby's and Colonel Campbell's columns. It was a long day, but an interesting one. As I rode over the ground I thought how splendidly our men had there behaved, especially Sergeant Ashfield and his twenty men, and regretted that no encouragement had been given them.

November 21st found us at Yservarkfontein near Bethel, the scene of another fight we had had under Colonel Benson. All the columns under General Bruce Hamilton were concentrating near Bethel. On the 22nd I rode over with Eustace to Bethel, and lunched with Colonel Campbell. Besides the colonel's column, there were here those of Colonels Allenby, Rawlinson, and Stewart. We heard at Bethel that that night there was some big move on, so leaving at 3.30 we hurried back, arriving at 5 p.m., and found that orders had just been issued for the column to be reorganised in three columns:—

Column A. Fit men and horses, 10 *per cent* spare horses, two days' rations, no transport.
Column B. Light transport with rations, escorted by infantry and men with weak horses.
Column C. Heavy baggage, infantry, and sick horses.

At 6 p.m. the mobile column "A" got orders to start at 7.30 p.m., and I left in it with my company, nearly ninety strong.

This idea of large bodies of mounted men, ready to go for a time without transport, was what we had long hoped to see carried out. We were all ready to face any discomforts in order to gain some real advantage, and started off at 7.30 that night, about 4000 mounted men; I for one, at any rate, being full of hope. I felt very sleepy after the long day, and had the greatest difficulty in keeping awake and sitting on my horse. Soon after starting we were joined by the other columns, and we all moved along the same road in an easterly direction.

Night-marches had with Colonel Benson been a specialty. Before starting each man was told the object of the march, so that all started keen. At every drift, wire fence, or other obstacle there was a staff officer to superintend. The column was frequently halted, and straggling reduced to a minimum, and connection was always systematically kept up. No dogs, no talking or smoking, no rattling of wheels or accoutrements was allowed. On this occasion, with a large force, these precautions were especially necessary, but possibly owing to the size of the force, there was considerable confusion.

On several occasions I had the whole of my company strung out as connecting files, and we found the greatest difficulty in keeping touch, owing to the dark, even with each other The leading column forged ahead without waiting, and stray men from columns in the rear kept pushing up from behind. There were many drifts, and the ground was boggy after the heavy rains. At one drift a long range 12-pounder gun got stuck. Men from all columns came crowding up, and soon there was chaos. Men were shouting "Hullo! who are you?" "What corps is this?" "Where are the Greys?" "Have you seen anything of the 18th Hussars?" "Who the devil are you?" and so on, and it was not possible to right this confusion before dawn.

We were left as escort to the gun; we got it out and pushed on, and as the sun rose I could see clouds of mounted men in front of us. There were a few Boers in the distance, and there was a little shooting going on, I had no idea what was happening, or what was intended, but in the end, after a march of thirty-five miles, we camped at De Witte Krans on the Klein Olifants River, thirty miles east of Bethel.

On November 23rd, in the afternoon, Colonel Campbell rode over from his column and saw our men, telling them he "was glad they had done so well at Baakenlaagte." This, coming from our own colonel, was very much appreciated. The next night also was wet and cold, and we felt it all the more from being short of blankets and rations. We started back rather miserable, and marched five miles on the road we had come by, joining our "B" column, which had reached this point after great difficulties with its transport Eventually we returned to our "C" column near Bethel, and arrived there on the 27th, glad to get back to the comparative comforts it afforded, but disappointed at the poor results of our labours.

After this the columns again separated. We trekked to Carolina, where we arrived on December 2nd, having made several night-marches and expeditions *en route*, but with poor results. At Carolina we got a convoy from Wonderfontein. We got into touch with Colonel Fortescue's column, and heard that Louis Botha with 1800 men was at Klipstapel, about fifteen miles off; that he had tried to make them attack our column, but that his Burghers, having had enough fighting at Itala and Baakenlaagte, had refused.

On the 4th we started for another night-march. The ground was difficult and the night dark, but the column, being anxious to surprise a farm before dawn, did not go slowly in front. At a boggy *spruit*

THE ADVENTURES OF TWO TROOPERS OF THE 19TH HUSSARS

I waited behind to superintend the putting out of connecting files. When this was done I cantered up to the head of my connecting files, and found that the corps in front had galloped on, and that we had lost touch. I galloped off into space, and was lucky in finding the troops in front about half-a-mile on. I got the leading file into touch, but just then, unfortunately, my old grey galloped into a barbed wire fence, and came head over heels on top of me, doubling me up and rolling on me in that position.

The doctor came up and helped me, but there was no ambulance, so that by the time the rear of the column came up I had to decide between being left on the *veldt* ten miles from Carolina, or doing at least another twenty miles on horseback. I decided on the latter course, and had a most unpleasant experience. The column caught one waggon and 100 cattle, but no Boers, and at 12.30 on the 5th we got back to Carolina where I was laid up for four days,

From the 9th to the 14th we were continually on the move, making long marches by day and by night, co-operating with Fortescue's column to the north and with those under General Bruce Hamilton from Ermelo. These operations resulted in considerable captures of Boers and stock. On the 15th we returned to Carolina. Four men (Livesay, Cherriman, Allen, and Shepherd), who had been wounded with Colonel Benson, rejoined us here, quite mended, and ready to try their luck again.

On the 17th went out with Woodmass (19th Hussars) to signal; got shot at, but no damage on either side. Our transport was at this time reduced to a minimum. All spare men and kits and all sick horses were left at Carolina, which now became our base. The men's kits were limited to one blanket (on horse), one waterproof sheet, one great coat, one pair socks, shirt and drawers (on waggon); 150 rounds were carried by each man. The saddles were stripped, and eight boxes of ammunition were carried on the waggons. Besides this supply I always had in my company two boxes (2200 rounds) of ammunition on a pack-horse.

The hard work, and especially the constant night-marches, told on the horses, and many of our most hardy ones gave out We were now reduced to eighty men mounted and forty dismounted. The rest of the battalion only numbered ninety all told, so that the 25th M.I. was reduced to the strength of one strong company.

On the 18th Lynes went sick, and did not return. I was myself, like the horses, beginning to show signs of wear, and began to think about a change. On the 19th we got news which filled us with hope. Botha was said to be at the Lakes south of Carolina. General Bruce Hamilton, with columns under Rawlinson, Plumer, Williams (Clements?), and Wing (who had succeeded Colonel Campbell, invalided), was going to attack him at dawn, while our column with Fortescue's, together about 900 mounted men, was to head him off from the north. We left just before dark (sixty of our men had been out all day) feeling quite keen and hopeful. The horses were as light as possible, the men only being allowed one blanket, and carrying 150 rounds of ammunition. Each company had a Scotch cart, with eight boxes of ammunition and three days' groceries.

The roads were heavy, and the carts got into difficulties. We had a long way to go before dawn, and did not wait for them. They were abandoned, and three of them (including ours) were taken by the Boers next morning. About 11 p.m. the moon set, and a storm coming on, it got very dark. It was impossible to tell whom one rode next to, so that at dawn the Scottish Horse, 3rd M.I., and Riflemen were all mixed up. I had just sorted my men with difficulty when we got the order to trot, then to gallop, and before I could stop it there was a stampede and chaos. I followed the stampede to a farm, whence we heard shooting in all directions, and didn't know what was going on.

All turned out well in the end; we took five wounded and eighteen unwounded prisoners, and a lot of horses and cattle. We had surprised Smit's commando at Lake Bannagher. Owing to the rain they had had no one on the lookout; 120 had got away. I thought it was a pity we had not surrounded the farm quietly. However, everyone was well pleased with what we had got, and we only knew of one of the Scottish Horse wounded and five missing. But poor Bramley, a great friend of mine, was one of the five missing. He had galloped on ahead with a few men, and got separated in the early morning mist. After taking one Boer prisoner, he was himself given no chance and shot from behind. He was reported missing for three days before we heard of his fate. This was the second good commanding officer lost by the Scottish Horse within two months.

We heard later that this commando had intended moving at 3 a.m., but had put it off owing to the bad weather. Louis Botha had left that night with the intention of going north. We made a short halt at Lake Bannagher, and after getting what breakfast we could in the heavy rain, moved back in good spirits, though cold and wet, to Bothwell on Lake Chrissie. The sun came out about 10 a.m. and dried and warmed us; we got a lot of pigs and chickens on the way. We camped on the same ground where General Smith-Dorrien had been attacked.

On December 21st, after a thirty-seven mile march, we had hoped to be able to rest our horses, but it was not to be, for at 9 a.m. next day the colonel got news of a Boer convoy which was reported to be trekking westwards, and by 9.30 all available mounted men were off after it. Our battalion luckily was advance guard, and about 11.30 a.m. we sighted the convoy about six miles off. I felt sure we should catch the convoy, but that the horses must suffer. We moved quickly, trotting and leading alternately, till we got to the point where we had first viewed the convoy. A few Boers shot at us, and I was told to reinforce White's company and push on. This we did together, and were very soon on the rearmost waggons, which were stuck in a *drift*.

A few shots did not delay us; we pushed on and spread panic into the Boers, who fled, leaving waggons and families, cattle and horses to their fate. We galloped on and on, past gesticulating families, broken-down waggons, and Boers waving their arms excitedly like windmills in token of surrender. We left all these to be dealt with in rear and pushed on. Once a Boer is on the run keep him on the run, was one of my maxims.

At last, however, after a nine-mile gallop, my pony was about done, and I only had four men up with me, so planting ourselves on a ridge, only one mile from the Klein Olifants River, between the Boers and a thousand of their cattle, we sat down, lit our pipes, and waited till more people should come up. Two or three Boers fired shots; we ran one down as he was shooting, but most of them cleared without firing. Soon, more men coming up under Eustace, they pushed on. There were only a few light carts left. Eustace pushed on well, and got all but two of the remaining carts, also a few more prisoners.

I could count sixty Boers escaping; there were quite enough to make it unpleasant for Eustace, with twenty-five men on beat horses, should they rally; so I sat down and watched, thinking I could do more good in the rear with fresh horses than in the front with beat ones if Eustace was followed up. We must have covered forty miles, and many of the horses were quite done for. Colonel Mackenzie decided to camp at Shapkraal, where the main part of the captured convoy was.

Seeing Eustace returning unmolested, I started back, and about three miles on found Colonel Mackenzie, who was very much pleased with the way our men had done. Everyone was pleased with our success. The total was a good one—twenty-three Boers, twenty waggons and twenty carts, besides many vehicles destroyed, about 2000 good cattle, and lots of trek oxen, horses and mules.

I had always been sceptical about the large hauls of waggons and stock so often reported in the papers, and it was hard to see how the Boers could hide so many waggons and such quantities of stock with so many of our columns at their heels, but in this case it was genuine enough.

The pace had told, and the column had many stragglers missing. Only one of our horses broke down, and that was Goldie's, which had got horse-sickness. He was one of our best men, and pluckily caught a wild two-year-old colt from a *Kaffir kraal*, saddled it up, and after three falls and a few sniping shots from Boers, rode it nine miles and joined us at Shapkraal. Others less resourceful and less lucky had to walk many miles, while a few were surrounded by Boers, taken and stripped, one or two being hit. Our men were lucky, for besides other loot we recovered our Scotch cart with its three days' groceries, a sack of coffee, and tins of milk. There were taken with the convoy chickens, turkeys, and ducks, besides bags of *mealie* meal, so that they all fared splendidly.

The Boers, to lighten their carts, had thrown away all sorts of things, and there were men walking about in frock coats and top hats and other Boer clothes. We also recovered a note-book belonging to Sergeant Ashfield, taken at Baakenlaagte, and a sword, probably Marsden's, taken at Dundee. I was on picquet that night with my company; it rained, and a plague of mosquitoes and sand-flies helped one to keep awake.

The next day, December 22nd, we retraced our steps, camping at Lillieput, which we did not reach till 8 p.m., owing to difficulties with the captured waggons over the boggy ground. The total results of the operations were:—

December 20th.—6 Boers killed, 2 wounded, 15 prisoners, 56 cattle, 150 horses, and 150 sheep.

December 22nd.—1 Boer killed, 20 prisoners, 24 waggons, 25 carts, 1000 cattle, 160 horses, and 800 sheep.

Colonel Mackenzie issued the following in orders:

The O.C. Column congratulates all concerned on the operations resulting in the capture of the Standerton commando's convoy. The 25th M.I. under Major Eustace, and particularly

Captain Crum's company, contributed in a marked way to the day's success. The O.C. Column believes that to the fact of moving with stripped saddles, though it entailed hardships and discomforts on all ranks for two days, it was due that over thirty miles were covered after a thirty-mile march in so short a time as five hours.

December 25th, our third Christmas Day on service, was an uneventful day; it rained hard. My company found the picquets, and we all got wet through. The turkey which we had captured with the convoy, and kept for this occasion, was unfortunately spoilt in the cooking. We spent the 24th and 25th at Klipstapel, the highest point in these parts, being at the source of the Vaal and Olifants Rivers. There was an extensive view from it, and it formed a good central position for operations against Botha, who was at this time not far off.

On the 26th we left Klipstapel. As usual we were seen off the premises by a few Boer snipers, but had no casualties, and returned to Carolina, where I sent in my application for leave home. I was sorry to take this step, as I should have liked to have seen the war out; but I felt that it might go on for a long time yet, and did not think that I could last much longer without a change. I had never felt quite the same since Baakenlaagte; my teeth gave me continual trouble, and in wet weather I suffered a lot with my arm. I had done four-and-a-half years in the country, and was getting stale and war-worn. On these grounds, and for family reasons, I felt justified in applying for leave. This leave was forwarded by Eustace, and also by General Alderson, who kindly removed all appearance of malingering by his complimentary recommendations.

On the 27th we were joined at Carolina by Hope, Wake, Marsh, and twenty men with some horses. In the afternoon there was a big storm. A cow and a horse were killed by lightning only twenty yards from Colonel Mackenzie's tent, a native with them escaping unhurt

On the 30th, at 6.30 p.m., we got short notice to start on a fourteen days' trek at 8 p.m. We had no idea why or where we were going. We marched all night—by the stars I could tell we were going east-south-east—and continued our march till 12 next day, when we reached Holnek on the road to Steynsdorp. The waggons got in at 3 p.m., having done thirty-four miles in nineteen hours, which was, I think, a very big march for transport. Sergeant Ross had gone to Pretoria on duty, so again I had Corporal Thompson as senior N.C.O. Here was a man who began the war as a lance-corporal now doing the work of a sergeant-major, and doing it well, with no extra pay, no crown on his arm, but with all the cares and responsibilities of the more exalted rank. Such cases were common throughout the army.

It turned out that we had been sent to block drifts over the Umpilosi River, while General Bruce Hamilton, with all his columns, came up to us from the south. This duty we performed until January 6th, when we started back to Carolina. These operations were a success, and resulted in the capture of General Erasmus and over 100 Boers.

The New Year opened with a lively fusillade at 6 a.m., some Boer snipers coming up in the mist and sniping into our camp.

On January 8th we returned to Carolina. On the 9th we found the picquets all round the camp, going out as usual half-an-hour before dawn. It was a very hot day till 3 p.m., when it became evident there was a storm coming. We got our horses in early from grazing, and had just watered and tied them up in the lines when the storm burst. A blast of wind and dust, then rain and hail. I ran to the lines and got some men out to stop the horses from stampeding.

We stood by them for a bit trying to quiet them, but the storm was too much for us. Hailstones and rain came down harder and harder, and for longer than I had ever seen. I never got such a hammering. We were driven back, and had to leave the horses to shift for themselves. My small tent was laid flat I crouched down in my oilskin and helmet, trying to save my neck and face at the expense of my hands. I got whack after whack on the knuckles and back from huge and sharp hailstones. I could just see that all the horses in camp were stampeding. No wonder, poor brutes; I would have stampeded myself if I had thought it would do me any good.

I fought my way backwards to the shelter of our mess tent, which was still standing. It was the fiercest of the many bad storms I have been in. Our men on Cossack-post had a bad time, with no shelter and most of their horses stampeded. After twenty minutes the hail gave place to a steady rain, and we all turned out to collect the horses. Watson was in great form, and worked like a trooper. Luckily there were two hours of daylight left, and a swollen river three miles from camp stopped the stampede, so that we recovered all but one of our horses, now reduced to seventy-three.

On the night of the 11th I did my last night-march. I do not know anything more trying than night-marches. One goes on and on, struggling to keep awake when the road is easy, and struggling to keep touch when it is difficult. Twenty-five miles is as much as you will do at a walk. If it is necessary to trot you are bound to have stragglers, and a straggler in the dark is as good as a man lost. At dawn one wakes up properly, and it is possible to get a good gallop out of the horses, but when the sun gets up, and it gets hot, men and horses begin to tire. You have shot your bolt, and though it may not have been successful it is not advisable to try it again.

Certainly it is a mistake to try on your beat horses to catch Boers on fresh ones. You will leave behind you many stragglers, will lose many horses from exhaustion—and will not catch the Boers. When the time comes for retiring it is odds on your having a nasty rear guard action on beat horses. On this occasion the columns under Williams and Wing from Ermelo, and we from Carolina, after long and well-timed marches, arrived at dawn on Klein Olifants River and captured forty-two Boers. But not content with this, on our return journey, the Scottish Horse and two of our companies started galloping after fifty Boers, They went for a long distance, did no good, and lost many men taken prisoners (including Eyre), and many horses from exhaustion.

We returned to Kromkrans, where we heard we were to be attacked at night by Botha. We dug good trenches, but had not the good fortune to be attacked when we were ready.

On the 14th we returned to Carolina, where we found Bircham, recovered from his wound. My leave had been granted on medical grounds, so after handing over the command to Bircham on the 15th, I said goodbye, to my great regret, to the oldest and best company of mounted infantry in the country.

Riding in to Wonderfontein, I took train to Middelburg. After a day or two there, and a short time in hospital at Pretoria, I found myself, on January 27th, travelling down in great comfort to Natal, *en route* for home, on the Princess Christian ambulance train.

Looking back on the war, and thinking of the "might-have-beens," many disappointments cropped up; but the joy of going home, with the feeling of having done one's share, outweighed all regrets, so that I travelled down from Pretoria with a lighter heart and far happier than I felt when, over two years before, I had travelled up on the same line in the Boer ambulance train. After a short stay at Howick with 1000 other invalids, I embarked on February 4th, 1902, at Durban, in the hospital ship s.s. *Avoca*.

In my anxiety to get home I feared all sorts of mishaps, but the

Avoca made no mistake, and on March 1st she did the 1000 invalids a real good turn by putting them down safely at Southampton Dock.

Thousands of men have come home from the war. Thousands of thousands rejoiced at the Declaration of Peace on June 1st, and many thousands shouted themselves hoarse as they welcomed Lord Kitchener home on July 12th. Let me only say here that of all those thousands not one was more enthusiastic or appreciative than myself. All these things have been fully and frequently described. My only excuse for writing this story is that it may throw side-lights on the history of the war which might not otherwise be seen.

ALSO FROM LEONAUR
AVAILABLE IN SOFTCOVER OR HARDCOVER WITH DUST JACKET

THE RELUCTANT REBEL by *William G. Stevenson*—A young Kentuckian's experiences in the Confederate Infantry & Cavalry during the American Civil War..

BOOTS AND SADDLES by *Elizabeth B. Custer*—The experiences of General Custer's Wife on the Western Plains.

FANNIE BEERS' CIVIL WAR by *Fannie A. Beers*—A Confederate Lady's Experiences of Nursing During the Campaigns & Battles of the American Civil War.

LADY SALE'S AFGHANISTAN by *Florentia Sale*—An Indomitable Victorian Lady's Account of the Retreat from Kabul During the First Afghan War.

THE TWO WARS OF MRS DUBERLY by *Frances Isabella Duberly*—An Intrepid Victorian Lady's Experience of the Crimea and Indian Mutiny.

THE REBELLIOUS DUCHESS by *Paul F. S. Dermoncourt*—The Adventures of the Duchess of Berri and Her Attempt to Overthrow French Monarchy.

LADIES OF WATERLOO by *Charlotte A. Eaton, Magdalene de Lancey & Juana Smith*—The Experiences of Three Women During the Campaign of 1815: Waterloo Days by Charlotte A. Eaton, A Week at Waterloo by Magdalene de Lancey & Juana's Story by Juana Smith.

TWO YEARS BEFORE THE MAST by *Richard Henry Dana. Jr.*—The account of one young man's experiences serving on board a sailing brig—the Penelope—bound for California, between the years 1834-36.

A SAILOR OF KING GEORGE by *Frederick Hoffman*—From Midshipman to Captain—Recollections of War at Sea in the Napoleonic Age 1793-1815.

LORDS OF THE SEA by *A. T. Mahan*—Great Captains of the Royal Navy During the Age of Sail.

COGGESHALL'S VOYAGES: VOLUME 1 by *George Coggeshall*—The Recollections of an American Schooner Captain.

COGGESHALL'S VOYAGES: VOLUME 2 by *George Coggeshall*—The Recollections of an American Schooner Captain.

TWILIGHT OF EMPIRE by *Sir Thomas Ussher & Sir George Cockburn*—Two accounts of Napoleon's Journeys in Exile to Elba and St. Helena: Narrative of Events by Sir Thomas Ussher & Napoleon's Last Voyage: Extract of a diary by Sir George Cockburn.

AVAILABLE ONLINE AT www.leonaur.com
AND FROM ALL GOOD BOOK STORES

ALSO FROM LEONAUR
AVAILABLE IN SOFTCOVER OR HARDCOVER WITH DUST JACKET

ESCAPE FROM THE FRENCH by Edward Boys—A Young Royal Navy Midshipman's Adventures During the Napoleonic War.

THE VOYAGE OF H.M.S. PANDORA by Edward Edwards R. N. & George Hamilton, edited by Basil Thomson—In Pursuit of the Mutineers of the Bounty in the South Seas—1790-1791.

MEDUSA by J. B. Henry Savigny and Alexander Correard and Charlotte-Adélaïde Dard —Narrative of a Voyage to Senegal in 1816 & The Sufferings of the Picard Family After the Shipwreck of the Medusa.

THE SEA WAR OF 1812 VOLUME 1 by A. T. Mahan—A History of the Maritime Conflict.

THE SEA WAR OF 1812 VOLUME 2 by A. T. Mahan—A History of the Maritime Conflict.

WETHERELL OF H. M. S. HUSSAR by John Wetherell—The Recollections of an Ordinary Seaman of the Royal Navy During the Napoleonic Wars.

THE NAVAL BRIGADE IN NATAL by C. R. N. Burne—With the Guns of H. M. S. Terrible & H. M. S. Tartar during the Boer War 1899-1900.

THE VOYAGE OF H. M. S. BOUNTY by William Bligh—The True Story of an 18th Century Voyage of Exploration and Mutiny.

SHIPWRECK! by William Gilly—The Royal Navy's Disasters at Sea 1793-1849.

KING'S CUTTERS AND SMUGGLERS: 1700-1855 by E. Keble Chatterton—A unique period of maritime history-from the beginning of the eighteenth to the middle of the nineteenth century when British seamen risked all to smuggle valuable goods from wool to tea and spirits from and to the Continent.

CONFEDERATE BLOCKADE RUNNER by John Wilkinson—The Personal Recollections of an Officer of the Confederate Navy.

NAVAL BATTLES OF THE NAPOLEONIC WARS by W. H. Fitchett—Cape St. Vincent, the Nile, Cadiz, Copenhagen, Trafalgar & Others.

PRISONERS OF THE RED DESERT by R. S. Gwatkin-Williams—The Adventures of the Crew of the Tara During the First World War.

U-BOAT WAR 1914-1918 by James B. Connolly/Karl von Schenk—Two Contrasting Accounts from Both Sides of the Conflict at Sea D uring the Great War.

AVAILABLE ONLINE AT www.leonaur.com
AND FROM ALL GOOD BOOK STORES

ALSO FROM LEONAUR
AVAILABLE IN SOFTCOVER OR HARDCOVER WITH DUST JACKET

IRON TIMES WITH THE GUARDS *by An O. E. (G. P. A. Fildes)*—The Experiences of an Officer of the Coldstream Guards on the Western Front During the First World War.

THE GREAT WAR IN THE MIDDLE EAST: 1 *by W. T. Massey*—The Desert Campaigns & How Jerusalem Was Won---two classic accounts in one volume.

THE GREAT WAR IN THE MIDDLE EAST: 2 *by W. T. Massey*—Allenby's Final Triumph.

SMITH-DORRIEN *by Horace Smith-Dorrien*—Isandlwhana to the Great War.

1914 *by Sir John French*—The Early Campaigns of the Great War by the British Commander.

GRENADIER *by E. R. M. Fryer*—The Recollections of an Officer of the Grenadier Guards throughout the Great War on the Western Front.

BATTLE, CAPTURE & ESCAPE *by George Pearson*—The Experiences of a Canadian Light Infantryman During the Great War.

DIGGERS AT WAR *by R. Hugh Knyvett & G. P. Cuttriss*—"Over There" With the Australians by R. Hugh Knyvett and Over the Top With the Third Australian Division by G. P. Cuttriss. Accounts of Australians During the Great War in the Middle East, at Gallipoli and on the Western Front.

HEAVY FIGHTING BEFORE US *by George Brenton Laurie*—The Letters of an Officer of the Royal Irish Rifles on the Western Front During the Great War.

THE CAMELIERS *by Oliver Hogue*—A Classic Account of the Australians of the Imperial Camel Corps During the First World War in the Middle East.

RED DUST *by Donald Black*—A Classic Account of Australian Light Horsemen in Palestine During the First World War.

THE LEAN, BROWN MEN *by Angus Buchanan*—Experiences in East Africa During the Great War with the 25th Royal Fusiliers—the Legion of Frontiersmen.

THE NIGERIAN REGIMENT IN EAST AFRICA *by W. D. Downes*—On Campaign During the Great War 1916-1918.

THE 'DIE-HARDS' IN SIBERIA *by John Ward*—With the Middlesex Regiment Against the Bolsheviks 1918-19.

AVAILABLE ONLINE AT **www.leonaur.com**
AND FROM ALL GOOD BOOK STORES

ALSO FROM LEONAUR
AVAILABLE IN SOFTCOVER OR HARDCOVER WITH DUST JACKET

FARAWAY CAMPAIGN by *F. James*—Experiences of an Indian Army Cavalry Officer in Persia & Russia During the Great War.

REVOLT IN THE DESERT by *T. E. Lawrence*—An account of the experiences of one remarkable British officer's war from his own perspective.

MACHINE-GUN SQUADRON by *A. M. G.*—The 20th Machine Gunners from British Yeomanry Regiments in the Middle East Campaign of the First World War.

A GUNNER'S CRUSADE by *Antony Bluett*—The Campaign in the Desert, Palestine & Syria as Experienced by the Honourable Artillery Company During the Great War.

DESPATCH RIDER by *W. H. L. Watson*—The Experiences of a British Army Motorcycle Despatch Rider During the Opening Battles of the Great War in Europe.

TIGERS ALONG THE TIGRIS by *E. J. Thompson*—The Leicestershire Regiment in Mesopotamia During the First World War.

HEARTS & DRAGONS by *Charles R. M. F. Crutwell*—The 4th Royal Berkshire Regiment in France and Italy During the Great War, 1914-1918.

INFANTRY BRIGADE: 1914 by *John Ward*—The Diary of a Commander of the 15th Infantry Brigade, 5th Division, British Army, During the Retreat from Mons.

DOING OUR 'BIT' by *Ian Hay*—Two Classic Accounts of the Men of Kitchener's 'New Army' During the Great War including *The First 100,000* & *All In It*.

AN EYE IN THE STORM by *Arthur Ruhl*—An American War Correspondent's Experiences of the First World War from the Western Front to Gallipoli-and Beyond.

STAND & FALL by *Joe Cassells*—With the Middlesex Regiment Against the Bolsheviks 1918-19.

RIFLEMAN MACGILL'S WAR by *Patrick MacGill*—A Soldier of the London Irish During the Great War in Europe including *The Amateur Army*, *The Red Horizon* & *The Great Push*.

WITH THE GUNS by *C. A. Rose & Hugh Dalton*—Two First Hand Accounts of British Gunners at War in Europe During World War 1- Three Years in France with the Guns and With the British Guns in Italy.

THE BUSH WAR DOCTOR by *Robert V. Dolbey*—The Experiences of a British Army Doctor During the East African Campaign of the First World War.

AVAILABLE ONLINE AT **www.leonaur.com**
AND FROM ALL GOOD BOOK STORES

ALSO FROM LEONAUR
AVAILABLE IN SOFTCOVER OR HARDCOVER WITH DUST JACKET

THE 9TH—THE KING'S (LIVERPOOL REGIMENT) IN THE GREAT WAR 1914 - 1918 by *Enos H. G. Roberts*—Mersey to mud—war and Liverpool men.

THE GAMBARDIER by *Mark Severn*—The experiences of a battery of Heavy artillery on the Western Front during the First World War.

FROM MESSINES TO THIRD YPRES by *Thomas Floyd*—A personal account of the First World War on the Western front by a 2/5th Lancashire Fusilier.

THE IRISH GUARDS IN THE GREAT WAR - VOLUME 1 by *Rudyard Kipling*—Edited and Compiled from Their Diaries and Papers—The First Battalion.

THE IRISH GUARDS IN THE GREAT WAR - VOLUME 1 by *Rudyard Kipling*—Edited and Compiled from Their Diaries and Papers—The Second Battalion.

ARMOURED CARS IN EDEN by *K. Roosevelt*—An American President's son serving in Rolls Royce armoured cars with the British in Mesopatamia & with the American Artillery in France during the First World War.

CHASSEUR OF 1914 by *Marcel Dupont*—Experiences of the twilight of the French Light Cavalry by a young officer during the early battles of the great war in Europe.

TROOP HORSE & TRENCH by *R.A. Lloyd*—The experiences of a British Lifeguardsman of the household cavalry fighting on the western front during the First World War 1914-18.

THE EAST AFRICAN MOUNTED RIFLES by *C.J. Wilson*—Experiences of the campaign in the East African bush during the First World War.

THE LONG PATROL by *George Berrie*—A Novel of Light Horsemen from Gallipoli to the Palestine campaign of the First World War.

THE FIGHTING CAMELIERS by *Frank Reid*—The exploits of the Imperial Camel Corps in the desert and Palestine campaigns of the First World War.

STEEL CHARIOTS IN THE DESERT by *S. C. Rolls*—The first world war experiences of a Rolls Royce armoured car driver with the Duke of Westminster in Libya and in Arabia with T.E. Lawrence.

WITH THE IMPERIAL CAMEL CORPS IN THE GREAT WAR by *Geoffrey Inchbald*—The story of a serving officer with the British 2nd battalion against the Senussi and during the Palestine campaign.

AVAILABLE ONLINE AT www.leonaur.com
AND FROM ALL GOOD BOOK STORES

ALSO FROM LEONAUR
AVAILABLE IN SOFTCOVER OR HARDCOVER WITH DUST JACKET

THE ART OF WAR by Antoine Henri Jomini—Strategy & Tactics From the Age of Horse & Musket

THE MILITARY RELIGIOUS ORDERS OF THE MIDDLE AGES by F. C. Woodhouse—The Knights Templar, Hospitaller and Others.

THE BENGAL NATIVE ARMY by F. G. Cardew—An Invaluable Reference Resource.

THE 7TH (QUEEN'S OWN) HUSSARS: Volume 4—1688-1914 by C. R. B. Barrett—Uniforms, Equipment, Weapons, Traditions, the Services of Notable Officers and Men & the Appendices to All Volumes—Volume 4: 1688-1914.

THE SWORD OF THE CROWN by Eric W. Sheppard—A History of the British Army to 1914.

THE 7TH (QUEEN'S OWN) HUSSARS: Volume 3—1818-1914 by C. R. B. Barrett—On Campaign During the Canadian Rebellion, the Indian Mutiny, the Sudan, Matabeleland, Mashonaland and the Boer War Volume 3: 1818-1914.

THE CAMPAIGN OF WATERLOO by Antoine Henri Jomini—A Political & Military History from the French perspective.

THE AUXILIA OF THE ROMAN IMPERIAL ARMY by G. L. Cheeseman.

CAVALRY IN THE FRANCO-PRUSSIAN WAR by Jean Jacques Théophile Bonie & Otto August Johannes Kaehler—Actions of French Cavalry 1870 by Jean Jacques Théophile Bonie and Cavalry at Vionville & Mars-la-Tour by Otto August Johannes Kaehler.

NAPOLEON'S MEN AND METHODS by Alexander L. Kielland—The Rise and Fall of the Emperor and His Men Who Fought by His Side.

THE WOMAN IN BATTLE by Loreta Janeta Velazquez—Soldier, Spy and Secret Service Agent for the Confederancy During the American Civil War.

THE MILITARY SYSTEM OF THE ROMANS by Albert Harkness.

THE BATTLE OF ORISKANY 1777 by Ellis H. Roberts—The Conflict for the Mowhawk Valley During the American War of Independenc.

PERSONAL RECOLLECTIONS OF JOAN OF ARC by Mark Twain.

AVAILABLE ONLINE AT www.leonaur.com
AND FROM ALL GOOD BOOK STORES

www.ingramcontent.com/pod-product-compliance
Lightning Source LLC
Chambersburg PA
CBHW021006090426
42738CB00007B/683